U.S. Fish & Wildlife Service

Rydell
National Wildlife Refuge

Comprehensive
Conservation Plan and
Environmental Assessment

I0415671

Rydell National Wildlife Refuge

Comprehensive Conservation Plan Approval
U.S. Fish and Wildlife Service, Region 3

Submitted by:

_____   9/21/01

Richard Julian   Date
Refuge Manager

Concur:

_____   9/27/01

Don Hultman   Date
Refuge Supervisor (RFS 3)

_____   9-29-2001

Nita M. Fuller   Date
Regional Chief
National Wildlife Refuge System

Approve: Marvin E. Moriarty
                 Acting Regional Director

_____   9/28/01

William F. Hartwig   Date
Regional Director

Acknowledgments

A variety of groups and individuals provided invaluable assistance with the preparation of this Comprehensive Conservation Plan. We gratefully acknowledge the input and support of:

Shawn Abraham
NRCS, McIntosh, Minnesota

Jack Bailey
Union/Sara Lake Campground

John Dobrovolny, USFWS
Regional Historic Preservation
Officer

Dave Fink
Water Programs Technician
Red Lake Watershed District

Paul Glander, Minnesota DNR
Area Fisheries Supervisor

Wayne Goeken
Development Director
Agassiz Environmental Learning
Center

Jay Johnson
Executive Director
Options Resource Center

Rick Julian, USFWS
Refuge Manager
Rydell National Wildlife Refuge

Allen Hanson, Minnesota DNR
Conservation Officer, Retired

Bob Hiltner, USFWS
Maintenance Worker
Rydell National Wildlife Refuge

Gary Huberty, Minnesota DNR
Fisheries

Donna Larson
Rydell NWR Volunteer Coordinator

Gary Lee
District Manager
East Polk County SWCD

Mike Marxen, USFWS
Landscape Architect/Planner

Jerry Paul, Minnesota DNR
Regional Hydrologist

Les Peterson, USFWS
Wildlife Biologist
Detroit Lakes WMD

Dave Radloff, USFWS
Fishery Biologist
Pendills Creek National
Fish Hatchery

Bill Roeszler
President
American State Bank

Rollin Siegfried, USFWS
When serving as Complex Manager
Minnesota Wetland Management
Complex

Chuck Schear
President
Mentor Sportman's Club

Dan Svedarsky
Professor of Natural Resources
University of Minnesota, Crookston

Rupert Syverson
Chairman
Polk County Board of Commissioners

Stephen Taylor
President
Fertile Community Conservation Club

Douglas Thorson
Board Member
Maple Lake Improvement District

Terry Wolfe, Minnesota DNR
Area Wildlife Manager
Crookston, Minnesota

Contents

Acknowledgments i

Chapter 1: Vision, Introduction and Background 1
A Vision for Rydell National Wildlife Refuge 1
Introduction 1
The U.S. Fish and Wildlife Service 2
The National Wildlife Refuge System 2
Purpose of Rydell National Wildlife Refuge 3
Existing Partnerships 5
Legal and Policy Guidance 5

Chapter 2: The Planning Process 6
Planning Issues 6
    Water Management 7
    Water Quality 7
    Community Involvement 7
    Public Use 7
    Interpretive and Educational Potential 7
    Habitat Restoration and Management 8

Chapter 3: The Refuge Environment 9
Geographic/Ecosystem Setting 9
    The Mississippi Headwaters/Tallgrass Prairie Ecosystem 9
Migratory Bird Conservation Initiatives 10
    Partners in Flight 10
    North American Waterfowl Management Plan 10
Detroit Lakes Wetland Management District 11
Region 3 Fish & Wildlife Resource Conservation Priorities 11
Refuge Resources, Cultural Values and Uses 12
    General 12
    Refuge Resources 12
        Major Habitats 12
        Plant Communities 13
        Wildlife 16
        Existing Facilities 16
        Cultural Resources 16
    Existing Programs 17
        Volunteers and Friends 17
        White-tailed Deer Management Hunt 17
        Visitor and Education Programs 18
        Fishery Management 19
        Cropland Management 19
        Cultural Resources Management 19
        Wilderness Review 20

Chapter 4: Management Direction **21**
Habitat Restoration and Wildlife Management 21
1.0 Habitat Restoration and Wildlife Management Goal: 23
        Potential Climate Change.. 29
Water Quality Management 30
2.0 Water Quality Management Goal: 30
Community Involvement 32
3.0 Community Involvement Goal: 32
Public Use 33
4.0 Public Use Goal: 34
5.0 Protection Goal: 37

Chapter 5: Plan Implementation **38**
Partnerships 38
Personnel Needs 39
Step-down Management Plans 39
Funding 40
Monitoring and Evaluation 40

Index **41**

Appendix A: Glossary **47**
Appendix B: Bibliography **53**
Appendix C: Chronology of Events **57**
Appendix D: Library Distribution **61**
Appendix E: Project List **65**
Appendix F: Species List **69**
Appendix G: Compliance Requirements **83**
Appendix H : Compatibility Determinations **89**
Appendix I: Environmental Assessment **111**
Appendix J: Mailing List **131**
Appendix K: List of Preparers **135**
Appendix K: Summary and Disposition of Public Comments on the Draft CCP . **139**

List of Figures
Figure1 National Wildlife Refuges and Waterfowl Production Areas 4
Figure 2 Waterfowl Production Areas and Easements Near Rydell NWR 13
Figure 3 Original Vegetation of Minnesota 14
Figure 4 Current Major Habitats 15
Figure 5 Planned Habitat Restoration and Management 24
Figure 6 Planned Water Management 27
Figure 7 Planned Water Quality Management 31
Figure 8 Planned Visitor Facilities 35
Figure 9 Current Staffing 39
Figure 10 Proposed Organization Chart 39

List of Tables
Table 1 Habitat Conversion.. 25

Chapter 1: Vision, Introduction and Background

A Vision for Rydell National Wildlife Refuge

Through innovative partnerships with multiple State and Federal agencies, conservation organizations and private individuals, Rydell National Wildlife Refuge will enhance habitat and populations of waterfowl, fish and other wildlife species; provide wildlife-dependent recreation; and demonstrate wildlife and natural resource conservation techniques. The majority of Refuge wetlands,

uplands, and woodlands will be restored and managed to reflect the original natural character of the landscape. Selected lakes will be managed to support waterfowl and fish. Trails, observation decks, a visitor center, a headquarters office and other facilities will be designed to provide enjoyable, informative and barrier-free wildlife-dependent experiences for people of all ages. The U. S. Fish & Wildlife Service and local citizens have charted a course of management for the Rydell National Wildlife Refuge that is designed to benefit wildlife and people well into the 21st century.

The charted course is described in this plan.

Introduction

Located in Polk County in northwestern Minnesota, Rydell National Wildlife Refuge is a 2,120-acre refuge that was established in 1992 on property donated to the U.S. Fish and Wildlife Service by the Richard King Mellon Foundation. The Refuge was established to protect wildlife habitat and diversity, to encourage waterfowl and other migratory bird production, and to promote environmental education and recreation. In addition, the Refuge was established to demonstrate sound fish and wildlife management and wise land and water stewardship.

This Comprehensive Conservation Plan, or CCP, will guide the development and management of the Refuge for the next 15 years (2001 through 2016).

The National Wildlife Refuge System Improvement Act of 1997 established clear legislative mandates for refuge management and planning, including:

- Wildlife has first priority in the management of refuges.

- Wildlife-dependent recreation involving compatible hunting, fishing, wildlife observation and photography, or environmental education and interpretation are the priority public uses of the Refuge System.

- Other uses have lower priority in the Refuge System and are only allowed if they are compatible with the mission of the Refuge System and with the purposes of the individual refuge.

Specifically, this Comprehensive Conservation Plan accomplishes the following objectives for Rydell National Wildlife Refuge:

- Provides a clear statement of the desired future condition of the Refuge.

- Ensures that management of the Refuge is consistent with the goals and policies of the National Wildlife Refuge System.

- Provides Refuge neighbors and partners with a clear understanding of the reasons for management actions on and around the Refuge.

- Provides for long-term continuity in Refuge management.

- Provides a basis for Fish and Wildlife Service staffing and for operation, maintenance, and capital improvement budget requests.

- Identifies potential projects for cost share and partnership contributions.

The U.S. Fish and Wildlife Service

> The mission of the U.S. Fish and Wildlife Service is to work with others to conserve, protect, and enhance fish, wildlife and plants and their habitats for the continuing benefit of the American people.
>
> *U.S. Fish and Wildlife Service (PL 105-57)*

By law and treaty, the Service has national and international management and law enforcement responsibilities for migratory birds, threatened and endangered species, fisheries and many marine mammals. The Service assists state and tribal governments and other Federal agencies in helping to protect America's fish and wildlife resources, and the National Wildlife Refuge System plays an important role in fulfilling many of these responsibilities.

The National Wildlife Refuge System

> The mission of the National Wildlife Refuge System is to administer a national network of lands and waters for the conservation, management and, where appropriate, restoration of the fish, wildlife and plant resources and their habitats within the United States for the benefit of present and future generations.
>
> *U.S. Fish and Wildlife Service*

The National Wildlife Refuge System is a network of more than 525 refuges encompassing 93 million acres of lands and waters, 41 wetland management districts that are responsible for 2.4 million acres of Waterfowl Production Areas, and 50 coordination areas covering 317,000 acres that are managed by State fish and wildlife agencies under cooperative agreements. Refuge System lands span the continent from Alaska's Arctic tundra to the tropical forests in Florida and from the secluded atolls of Hawaii to the moose-trodden bogs of Maine.

National wildlife refuges are established for different purposes. Most refuges have been established for the conservation of migratory birds while some have been established to provide habitat for endangered species; others have been formed to protect and propagate large mammals such as bison, elk, and desert bighorn sheep. Refuge habitats consist of a great diversity of plants and animals.

Within Minnesota, the Service manages 12 national wildlife refuges – Agassiz, Rydell, Hamden Slough, Crane Meadows, Tamarac, Big Stone, Rice Lake, Mille Lacs, Northern Tallgrass Prairie, Sherburne, Minnesota Valley, and Upper Mississippi River – and approximately 180,000 acres of Waterfowl Production Areas. (See Figure 1.)

Purpose of Rydell National Wildlife Refuge

The purpose of the Refuge arises from legislative authority. The Service acquired the property and established the Rydell National Wildlife Refuge under authority of the Fish and Wildlife Act of 1956, as amended, and the Recreational Use of Conservation Areas Act of 1962, as amended. Relevant sections from this legislation that establish the purpose of the Refuge include:

> "... for the development, advancement, management, conservation and protection of fish and wildlife resources... 16 U. S. C. 742f (a) (4) "... for the benefit of the United States Fish and Wildlife Service, in performing its activities and services. Such acceptance may be subject to the terms of any restrictive or affirmative covenant, or condition of servitude ..." 16 U. S. C. 742f(b) (1) (Fish and Wildlife Act of 1956, 16 U. S. C. 742(a) -764, as amended).

The Preliminary Management Plan, which accompanied the Environmental Assessment of the establishment of the Refuge, identified the Refuge's primary goal " to increase mallard, northern pintail, wood duck, redhead, canvasback, ring-necked duck and Canada goose production. Goals for these species are included in the Regional Resource Plan and the North American Waterfowl

Management Plan. Other migratory birds, endangered species, resident wildlife and associated habitats would also benefit from the broad based, diverse habitat management program (biodiversity)."

The Preliminary Management Plan identified the Refuge's secondary goal as a wildlife and fish management demonstration area "to provide the visiting public with opportunities to learn about effective fish and wildlife habitat management practices and land and water stewardship."

The Preliminary Management Plan raised the possibility of conducting aquaculture or fish hatchery operations for interpretative and educational purposes.

Figure 1: National Wildlife Refuges and Waterfowl Production Areas Within Minnesota

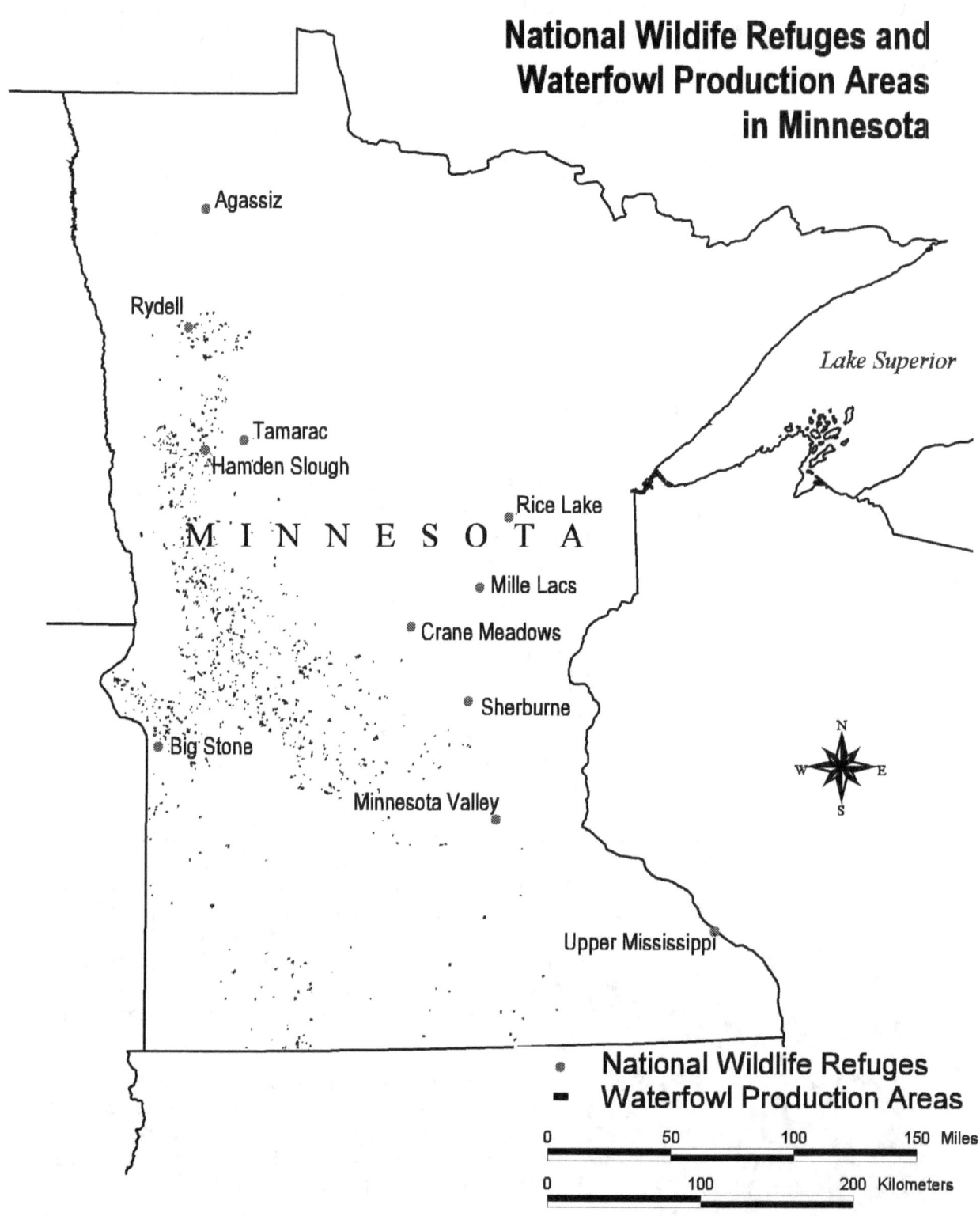

National Wildife Refuges and
Waterfowl Production Areas
in Minnesota

Agassiz

Rydell

Tamarac
Ham'den Slough

M I N N E S O T A

Rice Lake

Mille Lacs

Crane Meadows

Sherburne

Big Stone

Minnesota Valley

Upper Mississippi

Lake Superior

National Wildlife Refuges
Waterfowl Production Areas

| 0 | 50 | 100 | 150 Miles |

| 0 | 100 | 200 Kilometers |

Since the Refuge was established, the Refuge System Improvement Act of 1997 has further clarified the purposes of the Refuge System and refuges. The Act specifies that "each refuge shall be managed to fulfill the mission of the System, as well as the specific purposes for which the refuge was established." The Act further specifies that "compatible wildlife-dependent recreation is a legitimate and appropriate general public use of the System." Further, the Act establishes compatible wildlife-dependent recreational uses of hunting, fishing, wildlife observation and photography, and environmental education and interpretation as the priority general public uses of the System.

Existing Partnerships

Beginning with the Richard King Mellon Foundation's gift of the land and continuing through a variety of programs being offered today, partnerships have been a vital part of Rydell National Wildlife Refuge. The Friends of the Rydell Refuge Association, which formed in 1996, assists the Service with management, public use and fund raising activities. Other partners play a vital role in offering educational programs at Rydell. These organizations include:

- Options Resource Center for Independent Living
- Maple Lake Improvement District
- Union Lake Sarah Improvement Association
- Agassiz Environmental Learning Center
- East Polk County Soil and Water Conservation District
- Minnesota Department of Natural Resources

Former landowners continue to contribute to Refuge management and programming and are an invaluable asset to Rydell National Wildlife Refuge.

Legal and Policy Guidance

In addition to the Refuge's establishing authority legislation and the National Wildlife Refuge System Improvement Act of 1997, several Federal laws, executive orders, and regulations govern its administration. See Appendix G for a list of the guiding laws and orders.

Chapter 2: The Planning Process

The Service began developing the Rydell National Wildlife
Refuge Comprehensive Conservation Plan in June 1996, and
one of the first steps was to form a Citizen Committee that
would provide local and regional input to the plan. The
20-member group consisted of local residents, government
officials, individuals representing local business interests,
representatives from conservation and sportsmen's groups,
and representatives from educational institutions.

A kick-off workshop was held with the Citizen Committee
on June 11 and 12, 1996. Workshop participants identified
several management issues, concerns, and opportunities. A
public open house was also held on the evening of June 11 to
inform the general public of the planning process and to
gather individuals' ideas and concerns. Much of the information gathered from the public has been incorporated into
this Comprehensive Conservation Plan.

The Citizen Committee also met on September 19, 1996, and February 12, 1997.
Throughout the process, the Citizen Committee reviewed the components of the
plan and provided input into the process.

Additional meetings and discussions were held on water management and fishery
management.

Reference materials used in the preparation of the CCP include the Environmental Assessment prepared in 1991 during the establishment of the Refuge; the
vegetative survey report prepared in 1995; a Cultural Resource Overview study
prepared in 1997; the Polk County Comprehensive Local Water Management
Plan; aerial photographs; and numerous state and Federal maps. Much of the
information has been incorporated into a computerized geographic information
system. (A bibliography listing all of the resources used in preparation of this
Comprehensive Conservation Plan is included in Appendix B.)

Planning Issues

Issues, concerns, and opportunities were gathered in the first citizen and public
meetings and have been grouped together and summarized into major categories.
Issues are either occurring at the present time and need to be resolved or could
occur if the plan is implemented.

Water Management

Many of the lakes, wetlands, and water flows in the Refuge landscape have been altered over the years for fish rearing, farming, or aesthetic purposes. Most of the alterations were completed without permits or approval from the Minnesota Department of Natural Resources. Some people strongly favor restoring the hydrologic system on the Refuge to its original character. Removing all of the water control structures and channels on the Refuge, however, could limit some waterfowl management capabilities and hamper some fishery values demonstration opportunities. In addition, a county drainage ditch affects several wetlands on the Refuge.

Water Quality

Water quality within the Refuge, particularly in Tamarack Lake, is influenced by land management practices on lands draining into County Ditch 73. Water quality in Maple Lake, downstream of Tamarack Lake, is a major concern to local residents. Some people feel that potential projects could be identified to improve water quality and demonstrate effective water quality management practices on and off the Refuge.

Community Involvement

The local community is very interested in participating in the decisions that have an impact on the future direction of the Refuge. Former landowners, volunteers, and other individuals want to contribute and be involved in Refuge management and programs. The human history of the area (settlement, reliance on the land, structures) is of special interest and should play a role in the education and interpretation programs.

Public Use

Rydell National Wildlife Refuge presents a wide range of both issues and opportunities for Federal planners and the surrounding community. They include:

- Opinions vary on how to maintain the improvements made by the former owner, including trails, roads, observation structures, and buildings that provide visitor access to the Refuge.

- There is concern about the level of use that would be consistent with the natural resource values of the Refuge.

- Accessibility to the landscape, facilities, hunting and fishing, and other programs is a major concern.

Interpretive and Educational Potential

Most people support the concept of using Refuge resources and facilities to interpret the natural environment, educate about natural resources management, and demonstrate effective conservation techniques.

Habitat Restoration and Management

A wide range of habitat restoration and management decisions challenge Rydell National Wildlife Refuge, including:

- Control of exotic species such as Eurasian buckthorn, spotted knapweed, reed canary grass, and leafy spurge;

- Protection of unique natural communities such as the Sundew Bog, prairie remnants, and high quality maple/basswood forests;

- Limited habitat for forest interior species due to fragmentation of the existing forested habitat;

- Management and alteration of non-native plantings such as shelterbelts and conifer plantations; and

- Distribution and quantity of grassland, forest, and wetland habitat.

Chapter 3: The Refuge Environment

Geographic/Ecosystem Setting

The Mississippi Headwaters/Tallgrass Prairie Ecosystem

The U.S. Fish and Wildlife Service has adopted an approach to fish and wildlife conservation that is described as an ecosystem approach. What this means is that the Service is working to perpetuate dynamic, healthy ecosystems that ultimately will foster natural biological diversity. The strategy behind this effort is interdisciplinary and integrates the expertise and resources of all stakeholders.

Rydell National Wildlife Refuge lies within the Mississippi Headwaters/ Tallgrass Prairie Ecosystem. This ecosystem includes the majority of Minnesota and portions of Wisconsin and Iowa. The Ecosystem is one of transition from Prairie Parkland, to Eastern Broadleaf Forest, and then to Laurentian Mixed Forest. Land uses and conditions range from northern forests dominated by tourism and timber industries to vast areas of intensively used agricultural lands, typically containing severely fragmented and degraded remnants of the tallgrass prairie. A major threat to the Ecosystem is the continued loss and fragmentation of grassland, wetland and native woodland habitats for conversion to agricultural and other land uses. Degradation of remaining wetlands, lakes, and rivers due to runoff from agricultural lands and other non-point or point source discharges is also a concern. Timber harvesting, mineral extraction, and increasing pressures from recreational uses are problems in the northern reaches of the Ecosystem.

This Ecosystem supports neotropical and other migratory birds. It constitutes a key component of the Prairie Pothole Region, which produces 20 percent of the continental population of waterfowl. The Ecosystem supports several species of candidate and federally-listed threatened and endangered species including plants, mammals, birds, and mussels. No group of animals in the Midwest is in such grave danger of extinction as mussels. The four major watersheds of the Ecosystem (Mississippi, Minnesota, St. Croix, and Red rivers) are important habitats for these mussels and several species of interjurisdictional fishes such as the paddlefish and lake sturgeon.

The Service responsibilities must be accomplished in areas important to the state's economy. Agriculture provides a livelihood for one in four Minnesotans and the state ranks seventh in agricultural exports worth $2.4 billion. Minnesota's forested areas not only provide important wildlife habitat and stabilize soils but they also support a $7.8 billion forest products industry. Needs of citizens from rural, agricultural and forested areas of this ecosystem differ greatly from those of the Twin Cities, a major metropolitan area that is home to 2.2 million people.

Migratory Bird Conservation Initiatives

Partners in Flight

Nationally and internationally, several nongame bird initiatives are in the planning stage and implementation is expected to begin in the near future. Partners In Flight (PIF) is developing Bird Conservation Plans, primarily for landbirds, in numerous physiographic areas. The plans include priority species lists, associated habitats, and management strategies. The same elements will be by-products of ongoing planning efforts for shorebirds (U.S. Shorebird Conservation Plan) and colonial waterbirds (North American Colonial Waterbird Conservation Plan). As these plans are finalized, Rydell National Wildlife Refuge will strive to implement the conservation strategies they outline to the extent possible and practical.

Rydell National Wildlife Refuge lies within Partners in Flight Physiographic Area No. 40, Northern Tallgrass Prairie. Species priorities for this area can be found at http://www.cbobirds.org/pif/physios/40.html. The priority bird species for the grasslands/wetlands in Area No. 40 are Greater Prairie-Chicken, Nelson's Sharp-tailed Sparrow, Sedge Wren, Bobolink, and Yellow Rail. The priority bird species for riparian forest habitat is the Black-billed Cuckoo.

The Partners in Flight Plan for Physiographic Area No. 40 recommends that maintaining grassland/wetland complexes across the landscape is the most important factor necessary to maintain populations of birds in this suite. The plan recommends continuing the efforts to protect and restore wetlands in the Prairie Pothole Region, which will benefit priority non-game, wetland-associated birds. Due to the fragmented nature of grassland bird habitat, the Plan recommends providing large blocks of habitat as part of the grassland conservation objectives. The Plan proposes Bird Conservation Areas consisting of a 2,000-acre core of high quality grassland embedded in a 10,000-acre buffer. This buffer would include an additional 2,000 acres of smaller patches of grassland. (http://www.blm.gov/wildlife/pl_40sum.htm).

It is hoped that at some future point all bird conservation programs will be integrated under the umbrella of the North American Bird Conservation Initiative. This is a continental effort to have all bird initiatives operate under common Bird Conservation Regions, and for the people implementing these initiatives to consider the conservation objectives of all birds together to optimize the effectiveness of management strategies.

North American Waterfowl Management Plan

Signed in 1986, the North American Waterfowl Management Plan (NAWMP) outlines a broad framework for waterfowl management strategies and conservation efforts in the United States, Canada, and Mexico. The goal of the NAWMP is to restore waterfowl populations to historic levels. The NAWMP is designed to reach its objectives through key joint venture areas, species joint ventures, and state implementation plans within these joint ventures.

Rydell is within the U.S. Prairie Pothole Joint Venture (PPJV) area. The emphasis of the PPJV is to increase waterfowl populations through habitat conservation projects across the landscape. The philosophy of the PPJV is to accomplish projects at the local level through Federal partnerships with state and local governments, private organizations, and individuals. Through 1999, the PPJV had protected 558,420 acres of habitat, restored 223,107 acres, and enhanced 568,357 acres. Increasingly, the PPJV is cooperating in projects that will benefit shorebirds and grassland birds.

Detroit Lakes Wetland Management District

Rydell National Wildlife Refuge is located within the Detroit Lakes Wetland Management District. The District includes Becker, Clay, Mahnomen, Norman, and Polk counties. The Wetland Management District staff manage Waterfowl Production Areas and easements.

Waterfowl Production Areas preserve wetlands and grasslands critical to waterfowl and other wildlife. These public lands, managed by the U.S. Fish and Wildlife Service, became part of the National Wildlife Refuge System in 1966 through the National Wildlife Refuge Administration Act.

Wetland Management District staff also manage wetland easements; perpetual contracts with willing private landowners that protect their wetlands from draining and filling with soil. In recent years, grassland easements have been purchased to provide permanent grassland cover around wetlands to meet the needs of upland nesting waterfowl and other wildlife.

The District currently manages 40,489 fee acres on 155 Waterfowl Production Areas, and 306 easements covering 11,960 acres. In addition, 14 Conservation Easements totaling 1,340 acres are administered by the District, covering restored wetlands and farmed lands on former Farmers Home Administration inventory property.

Region 3 Fish & Wildlife Resource Conservation Priorities

The Government Performance and Results Act (GPRA) required the U.S. Fish and Wildlife Service to identify its most important functions and to direct its limited fiscal resources toward those functions. From 1997 to 1999 within Region 3, a group looked at how best to identify the most important functions of the Service within the region.

The group chose to focus on species in identifying conservation priorities. Group members prioritized species based on biological status (endangered or threatened, for example), rare or declining levels, recreational or economic value, or "nuisance" level. The group pointed out that species not on the prioritized list are important too. But, when faced with the needs of several species, the Service should emphasize the species on the priority list.

Refuge Resources, Cultural Values and Uses

General

Rydell National Wildlife Refuge is located in Grove Park and Woodside townships in Polk County, Minnesota, just south of U.S. Highway 2 between the communities of Mentor and Erskine. The Refuge is located between the flat Red River Valley floodplain on the west and the rolling hardwood forest and lake region on the east.

The Refuge is located on the eastern edge of the Lake Agassiz Plain subsection of the Red River Valley section of the ecological units of the Eastern United States. The potential natural vegetation types for the general area include bluestem prairie, northern flood plain forest along major tributaries of the Red River and, to the east, aspen parkland, dogwood-willow swamp, sedge meadow, big bluestem-Indiangrass prairie, bur oak openings-woodland, and maple-basswood forest.

Historically, bison and elk lived in the area. The dominant large predator was the wolf. Other species included prairie chicken, sharptail grouse, beaver, and meadow lark. The area supported large populations of nesting and migrating waterfowl. Major natural disturbances to the area included fire and high winds. Past changes by humans have included clearing of the land for agriculture, drainage of wetlands, logging, and the near-extinction of some fur-bearing mammals for the fur trade. Today, farming and recreation are the major human activities affecting the ecosystem.

The Refuge is part of the chain of national wildlife refuges that extends across Minnesota from the southeast to the northwest. It is also near the northernmost extent of waterfowl production areas that are scattered throughout western Minnesota. Numerous waterfowl production areas are located within 5 miles of the Refuge. (See Figure 2.)

At least 19 farmsteads existed historically within the Refuge boundaries. These farmsteads had been consolidated into one ownership by the time it was acquired by the Richard King Mellon Foundation in 1992. In the same year, the Foundation donated the property to the U.S. Fish and Wildlife Service to be managed as part of the National Wildlife Refuge System. The Refuge currently has two employees and is supported by administrative personnel of Hamden Slough National Wildlife Refuge.

Refuge Resources

Historically, the area in which the Refuge is located was a small forested island within the Prairie Pothole Region. A concentration of lakes south and west of the Refuge formed a "fire shadow" that supported the growth of maple-basswood and oak forest surrounded by northern tallgrass prairie. (See Figure 3, Original Vegetation of Minnesota.)

Major Habitats

Many of the trees were cleared for farming during the homesteading era. The areas that were not cleared were grazed. Today the Refuge is a mosaic of wetlands, hardwood stands, conifer plantations, grass meadows and cropland. Lakes and wetlands make up 570 acres of the Refuge; trees and shrubs about 554 acres;

Figure 2 Waterfowl Production Areas and Easements Near Rydell NWR

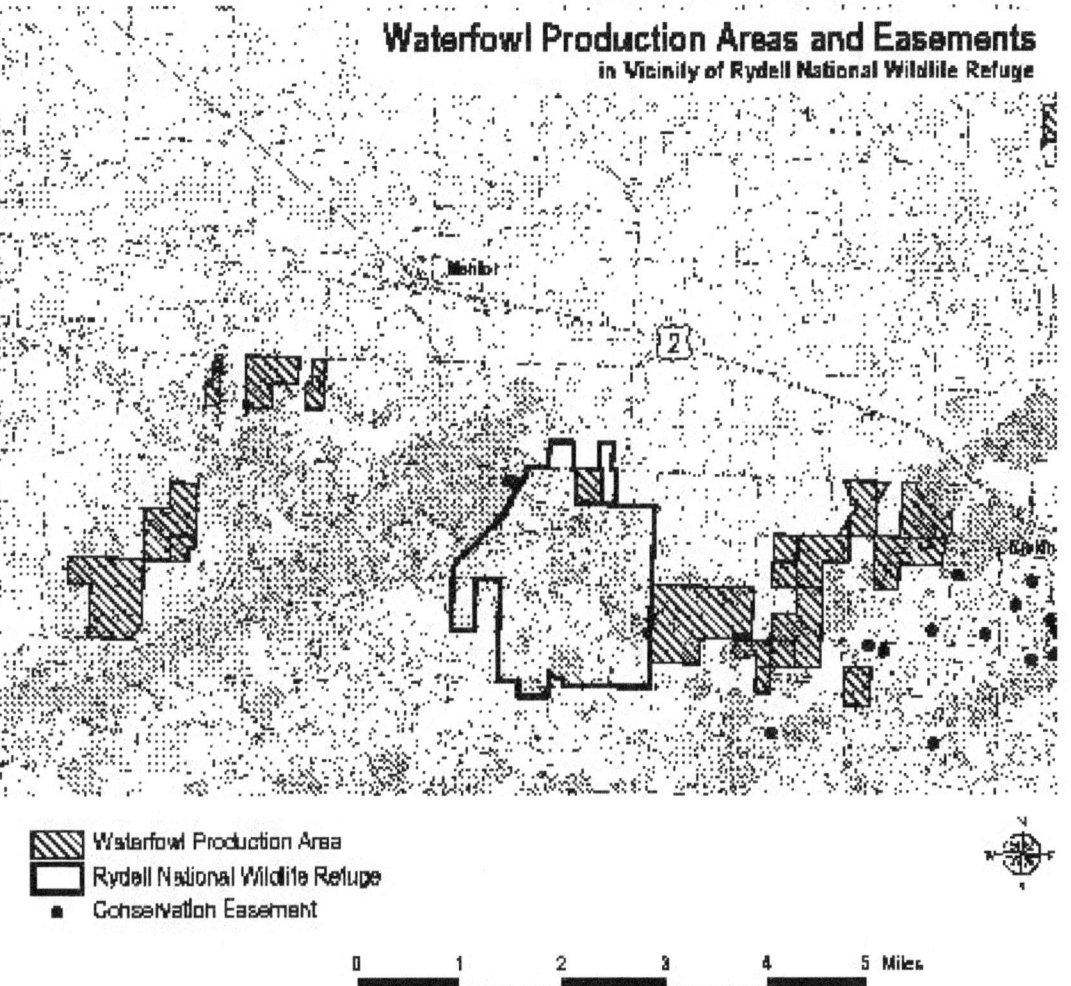

Waterfowl Production Areas and Easements
in Vicinity of Rydell National Wildlife Refuge

Waterfowl Production Area
Rydell National Wildlife Refuge
• Conservation Easement

0   1   2   3   4   5 Miles

grassland 489 acres; and cropland constitutes 272 acres (see Figure 4). The fragmentation of the plant communities negatively affects wildlife and ecosystem management. The area around the Refuge is dominated by agriculture with crops grown on most cleared land.

Plant Communities

In 1994 and 1995, a team of biologists from the University of Minnesota-Crookston conducted a baseline plant inventory with emphasis on native, remnant communities. The biologists concluded that "... the Refuge is in a uniquely positioned ecotonal setting on the borders of major North American biomes. Consideration should be given to looking at the entire Refuge as an example of large scale ecosystem restoration with a view towards restoring a sizable unit of maple-basswood and oak forest types, particularly for forest interior species (birds and plants)." Forest interior bird species are those that require large, unfragmented blocks of forest habitat. These species generally have been shown to be in decline due to pressures caused by increased predation and also nest parasitism by brown-headed cowbirds. The biologists further identified Sundew Bog as the most unique remnant community on the Refuge. The biologists also recommended controlling undesirable invasive woody species such as common buckthorn and prickly ash to protect the integrity of the native communities.

Figure 3: Original Vegetation of Minnesota

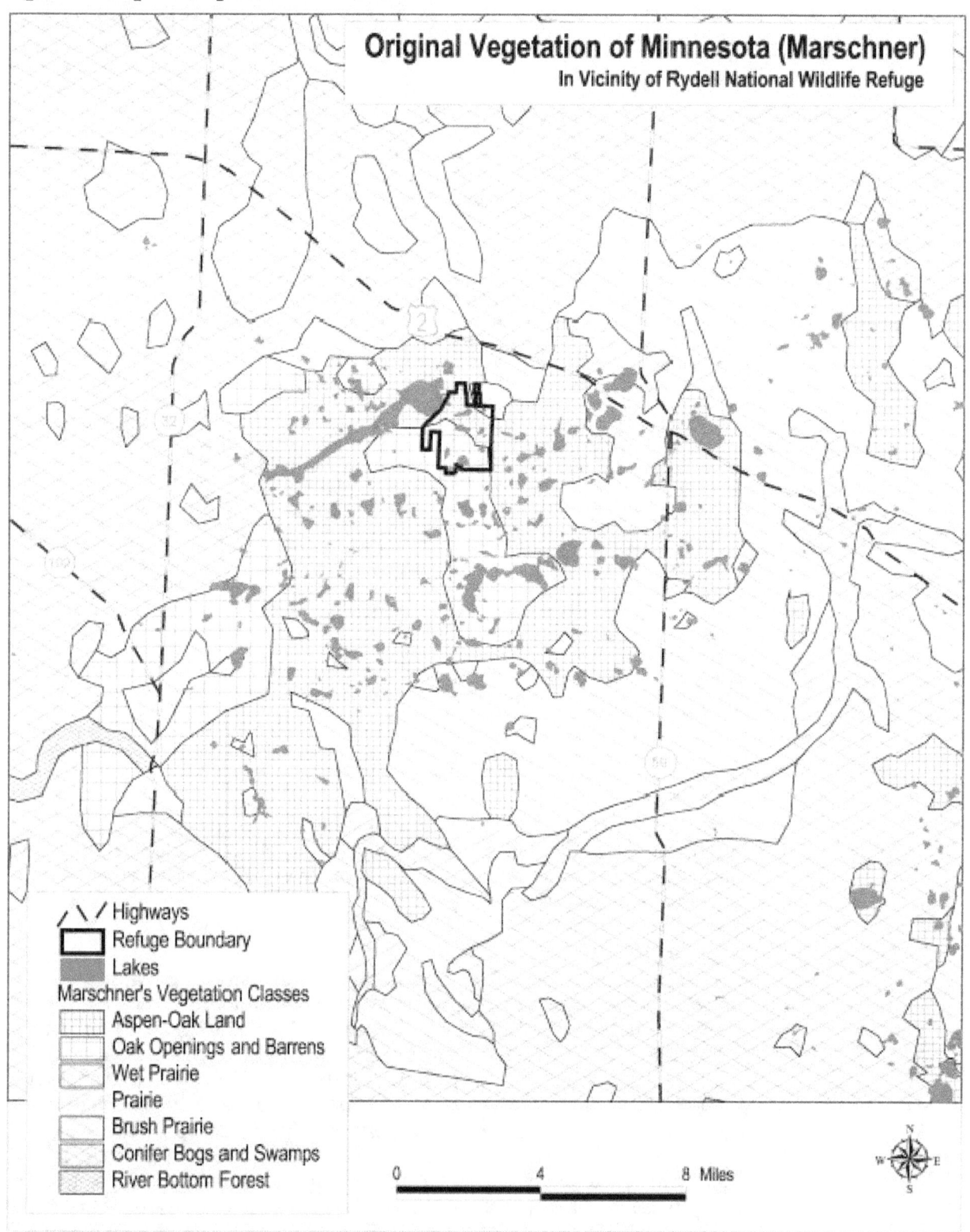

Original Vegetation of Minnesota (Marschner)
In Vicinity of Rydell National Wildlife Refuge

Legend:
- Highways
- Refuge Boundary
- Lakes

Marschner's Vegetation Classes
- Aspen-Oak Land
- Oak Openings and Barrens
- Wet Prairie
- Prairie
- Brush Prairie
- Conifer Bogs and Swamps
- River Bottom Forest

0   4   8 Miles

Figure 4: Current Major Habitats

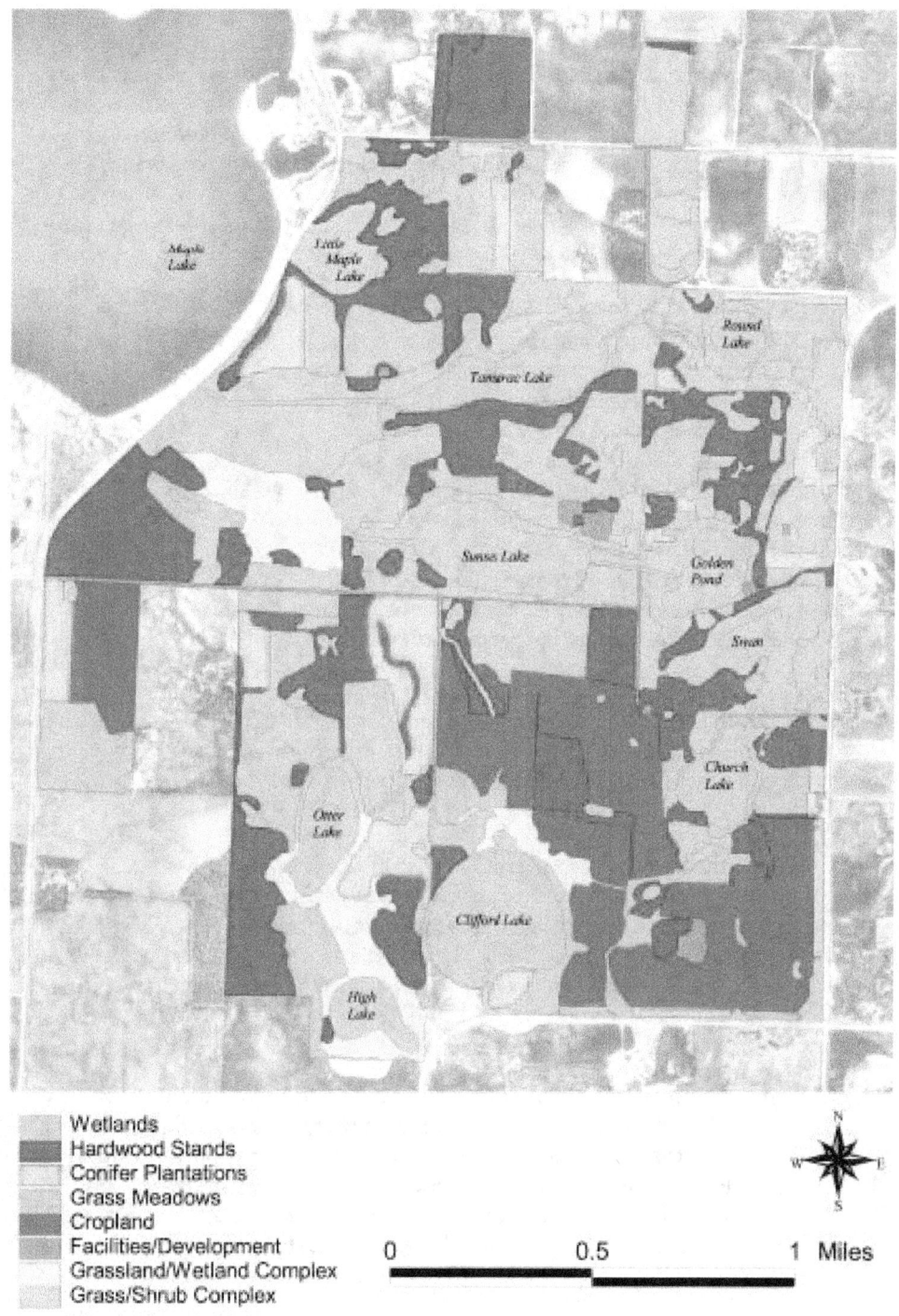

Wetlands
Hardwood Stands
Conifer Plantations
Grass Meadows
Cropland
Facilities/Development
Grassland/Wetland Complex
Grass/Shrub Complex

0   0.5   1   Miles

Wildlife

The diverse Refuge habitat is currently used by both diving and dabbling ducks, geese, swans, white-tailed deer, moose, ruffed grouse, cormorants, herons, rabbits, raccoon, otter, beaver, mink, muskrats, fox, coyotes, black bear, hawks, and owls. More than 195 species of birds have been observed on the Refuge (see Appendix F for a list of birds, reptiles and amphibians, mammals and butterflies). A bald eagle's nest is located approximately 1 mile south of the Refuge, and eagles and osprey are often seen using Refuge habitat. Trumpeter swans, a state-listed threatened species, were recently reintroduced on the Refuge and now use the Refuge regularly. The Refuge is within the peripheral range of the gray wolf and confirmed sightings of wolves have been reported on the Refuge.

Existing Facilities

The facilities on the Refuge include the Refuge office, a residence, a Visitor Center, a maintenance shop, two cold storage buildings, a small barn, a fish hatchery building, two earthen fish rearing ponds, three homestead sites with log structures, and a number of old buildings on former building sites. Several power lines transect the Refuge. The townships have abandoned all of their former roads within the Refuge, and these former roads are closed to the public. Approximately 9 miles of hiking/cross-country skiing trails were developed on the Refuge by the former owner.

We have discontinued use of the fish hatchery. The hatchery equipment, including tanks and fish fry hatching equipment, were transferred to the LaCrosse Fishery Resources Office. Walleye fingerling production will continue in one Refuge wetland to support Fish and Wildlife Service programs off the Refuge.

Cultural Resources

Responding to the requirement in the law that comprehensive conservation plans will include "the archaeological and cultural values of the planning unit," the Service contracted for a cultural resources overview study of Rydell National Wildlife Refuge. This section of the CCP derives mostly from the report, "A Cultural Resources Management Plan for the Rydell National Wildlife Refuge, Polk County, Minnesota," by Jeanne Ward and Robert Cromwell, Institute for Minnesota Archaeology, dated October 1997.

The Refuge has 24 reported cultural resources sites and 58 standing structures on Refuge land. Ward (1997:24) identified land characteristics on the Refuge indicative of prehistoric occupations; but Ward's areas of high potential shown on the map exclude the location of the one known prehistoric site on the Refuge. Ward studied several historic maps to determine the locations of previous and existing farmsteads and the school; but Ward's map locates no historic site at No. 9 (Gran). A historic farmstead at No. 3 (Raymond) is more problematic.

The potential for additional cultural resources on the Refuge is mixed. Undiscovered prehistoric sites are likely, especially for the Woodland culture (600 B.C. to A.D. 1650) in this vegetative transition zone. The Cheyenne tribe is the earliest historic period tribe in the area, replaced by the Ojibwa. Most likely all historic period sites have been located, with little potential for Indian sites and trading posts.

As of September 6, 2000, Polk County contains six properties on the National Register of Historic Places. All these properties are historic period structures located in cities.

Ward identified potentially interested parties. The Cheyenne, whose antecedent may have been the prehistoric Cambria culture, are not concerned about cultural properties in the Refuge area. By the early 17th century Dakota groups occupied the area, but similarly are not concerned about the Refuge area. Eventually the Ojibwa became the dominant tribe in the area, but only the Red Lake Band of Chippewa Indians now expresses an interest in cultural properties on the Refuge. No evidence exists for the removal of human remains from the Refuge area. The Polk County Historical Society has an interest in cultural resources on the Refuge. Thus, these two organizations should be consulted in the search for and evaluation of cultural properties on the Refuge.

Existing Programs

When established in 1992, the Refuge was managed by the Detroit Lakes Wetland Management District staff and one permanent Refuge employee. The Refuge now has an on-site manager and a maintenance worker. In the Refuge's first 8 years, several management emphases have emerged.

Public uses are a significant component of the Refuge's programs. All Refuge public use activities must be compatible with the National Wildlife Refuge System mission or the purposes of the Refuge. Wildlife-dependent recreational activities are compatible at Rydell. We determined that other activities are not appropriate at Rydell. These activities include the picking of wild flowers, recreational riding of all-terrain vehicles and snowmobiles, horseback riding, in-line skating, canoeing, beekeeping, fish bait harvest, and large-scale production of crops.

Volunteers and Friends

The volunteer program on the Refuge has developed and increased each year since 1992. In 1992, one volunteer contributed 320 hours of service; nine volunteers put in 373 hours in 1993; 26 people contributed 770 hours in 1994; 43 volunteers contributed 1,052 hours in 1995; 99 volunteers contributed 5,438 hours in 1996; and 164 volunteers contributed 5,455 hours in 1997. In 1998 and 1999, several volunteers logged more than 1,000 hours and one logged more than 1,500 hours. Many of the Refuge programs are possible only through the assistance of dedicated volunteers. The volunteer program is expected to grow and play an integral role in Refuge management.

The Friends of the Rydell Refuge Association was formed in 1996 to assist the Refuge with management, public use, and fund raising activities. The Friends Association received its nonprofit 501(c)(3) status in early 1997 and has begun applying for grant and aid monies to complete needed wildlife and public use projects. In 2000, the Association was awarded the Friends Association of the Year Award by the National Fish and Wildlife Foundation and the National Refuge Association.

White-tailed Deer Management Hunt

The Refuge and surrounding area historically attracted large numbers of deer, especially in winter, because both prairie and woodland habitat were available. The previous owner of the Refuge property actively encouraged deer to use the area by planting many acres of lure crops, limiting hunting pressure, and providing a high degree of protection for the deer herd. Because of this, the deer population increased dramatically and became concentrated in the relatively small area of the Refuge.

In 1993, the Refuge and surrounding area supported about 300 white-tailed deer in the spring and fall and about 800 in the winter. Over-population by deer was obvious. Browse lines in Refuge woodlands was evident and extensive crop damage occurred annually-both on farmed Refuge land and on neighbors' land.

To reduce the damage to Refuge vegetation and neighbors' crops, all of the lure crops were discontinued on the Refuge in 1994 and several corn plots were established on private or Federal lands within a 5-mile radius of the Refuge.

In addition, antlerless deer hunts were held on the Refuge starting in November 1994. During the next 3 years, 186 antlerless deer were taken on the Refuge through the management hunt.

Because the deer herd had been reduced sufficiently, two new deer hunts were conducted on the Refuge in 1996 – one for people with disabilities and one for youth. Both were conducted in accordance with the Rydell Deer Hunting Plan. The hunt by persons with disabilities was conducted on October 18 and 19 with the cooperative assistance of the Options Resource Center for Independent Living from East Grand Forks, Minnesota, and numerous volunteer hunting assistants. Twenty-three hunters harvested 11 deer. The deer hunt for youth ages 12 through 15 was conducted on November 9 and 10 with the cooperative assistance of the Minnesota Department of Natural Resources and 30 volunteer mentors. Thirty youth hunters participated in the training and hunting and 23 harvested a deer on the Refuge.

The winter of 1998 caused a significant reduction in the Refuge deer herd. Because of the reduced population, the only hunters permitted between 1998 and 2000 were persons with disabilities. In 1998, 17 hunters harvested seven deer. In 1999, 20 hunters harvested 12 deer. In 2000, 18 disabled hunters harvested 14 deer.

Visitor and Education Programs
In cooperation with the Friends of Rydell Association, the Maple Lake Improvement District, the Union Lake Sarah Improvement Association, the Agassiz Environmental Learning Center, and numerous volunteers, several wildlife-oriented public programs were initiated on the Refuge during 1996. The programs covered bluebird houses, landscaping for wildlife, bats and astronomy. Most of the programs were well attended and they have been expanded over the years.

On August 18, 1996, a "homecoming" open house was held on the Refuge. The event was open to the general public, and individuals who formerly lived on the land that is now refuge received special invitations. More than 290 people attended the event, many of whom had ties with former homesteading families on

the Refuge. Refuge auto tours, a historical program and exhibits were available for visitors to enjoy during the day. We have continued to host an annual Refuge open house since 1996.

Conservation tours for youth from several East Polk County school districts have been hosted by the Refuge and the East Polk County Soil and Water Conservation District during the past several years. About 180 seventh graders from four schools participate in the program each year. These programs are expected to continue.

With the help of dedicated volunteers, in June of 1996 the Refuge was opened to the public from 1 to 4 p.m. on Sundays. Since then the program has expanded to 12 to 5 p.m. each Sunday, year round. Volunteers answer questions, work around the Visitor Center and direct visitors to hiking trails. For the summer of 2000, we hired a student to keep the visitor center open from 12 to 5 p.m. Thursday, Friday, and Sunday and from 10 a.m. to 5 p.m. on Saturday.

Fishery Management
Each year, walleye fry supplied by the Minnesota Department of Natural Resources are stocked in Clifford Lake. The purpose is to produce advanced fingerling walleye to help meet the annual Fish and Wildlife Service fishery goals. The fingerlings are trapped in the fall to stock lakes on Region 3 National Wildlife Refuges and Tribal lands.

Cropland Management
Approximately 800 acres, or 37 percent of the Refuge, was farmed or hayed under a cooperative agreement with local farmers when the Refuge was established in 1992. The intent of the original farming program was to provide food plots for the wintering deer herd on the acquired land. After the Refuge was established, the cooperative farming agreement allowed the co-op farmer to use Refuge lands for crop and hay production in exchange for planting food plots on private property within 5 miles of the Refuge. This program was significantly reduced as the Refuge wintering deer population decreased to an acceptable level. Today 272 acres are still being farmed. Five hundred acres have been converted from tilled land to prairie, wetland, and forest restoration areas. The majority of the remaining cropland will be converted to grassland or wetland over the next 3 years.

Cultural Resources Management
The Refuge Manager considers potential impacts of management activities on historic properties, archeological sites, traditional cultural properties, sacred sites, and human remains and cultural materials. The Refuge Manager informs the Regional Historic Preservation Officer early in the planning stage to allow qualified analysis, evaluation, consultation, and mitigation as necessary.

The Refuge has no museum nor on-refuge museum collections (art, ethnography, history, documents, botany, zoology, paleontology, geology, environmental samples, artifacts). If an on-refuge museum were to be established, it would be required to adhere to 411 DM. To date, two cultural resources investigations have produced artifacts from Refuge lands; these collections are stored at the Minnesota Historical Society under a cooperative agreement.

Archeological investigations and collecting are performed only in the public interest by qualified archeologists working under an Archaeological Resources Protection Act permit issued by the Regional Director. Refuge personnel take steps to prevent unauthorized collecting by the public, contractors, and Refuge personnel. Violations are reported to the Regional Historic Preservation Officer.

Wilderness Review

As part of the CCP process, we reviewed the lands within the legislative boundaries of Rydell National Wildlife Refuge for wilderness suitability. No lands were found suitable for designation as Wilderness as defined in the Wilderness Act of 1964. Rydell National Wildlife Refuge does not contain 5,000 contiguous roadless acres nor does the Refuge have any units of sufficient size to make their preservation practicable as Wilderness. The lands of the Refuge have been substantially affected by humans.

Chapter 4: Management Direction

This section presents long-term guidance (15-year plan) for the Refuge in the form of Refuge goals, objectives, and strategies. This section is organized into four broad areas:

- Habitat restoration and wildlife management
- Water management
- Community involvement
- Public use and demonstration

For the purpose of this analysis, Refuge goals are qualitative statements that define what the Refuge must be to satisfy its purpose, legal mandates, and the needs of citizens and agencies having a vital interest in what and how the Refuge performs. The objectives provide quantitative bench marks that indicate progress toward the Refuge purpose and goals. Strategies are the specific actions and projects that will lead to the accomplishment of the management objectives.

The Refuge was donated to the U.S. Fish and Wildlife Service by the Richard King Mellon Foundation in 1992 to protect its valuable habitat and wildlife diversity, encourage waterfowl and other migratory bird production, provide wildlife-oriented recreation, and promote environmental education that is focused on demonstrating sound fish, wildlife, and agricultural practices. These purposes provide the basic framework for setting refuge goals, objectives, and strategies. Management functions, public uses, and facilities can be developed and provided only if they fall within the framework of and are compatible with the Refuge purpose. As such, a compatibility determination is the primary statutory standard determining which uses will be permitted on national wildlife refuge lands. All proposals in this plan are considered compatible based on a site-specific evaluation of the anticipated impacts (conflicts) on migratory bird use and habitat. See Appendix H for compatibility statements.

Habitat Restoration and Wildlife Management

Habitat restoration and wildlife management on the Refuge involves using a variety of management techniques to preserve, restore, and enhance the wetland, grassland, woodland, and other habitats for wildlife. Wetland management involves restoring drained wetlands and managing lake water levels to meet the

Guiding Principles of Management Rydell National Wildlife Refuge

Protect Wildlife

This includes all "hands-on" biological activities such as surveying and monitoring wildlife and habitat; relocating and reintroducing wildlife where appropriate; controlling populations of invasive destructive wildlife; preventing outbreaks of disease; responding to outbreaks when they occur; and preventing harmful population imbalances.

Improve Habitat

Improving habitat encompasses the full range of natural environmental management, from protection of pristine areas with little or no intervention in the natural process to intensive manipulation of soils, water, topography and vegetative cover. It includes restoration, enhancement, and management of wetlands, forests, grasslands, and other areas on the Refuge. Management strategies would include prescribed burning, wildlife-oriented farming, haying and grazing, control of invasive alien plants, and protection and monitoring of air and water quality.

Serve People

All of the educational and recreational activities that take place on the Refuge, as well as outreach ventures that occur elsewhere on behalf of the Refuge, relate to this guiding principle. Involving people includes all activities that are based upon contacts with people, such as the volunteer program and partnerships with organizations and individuals; law enforcement; Friends of the Refuge; and Refuge visitors. It also includes management of archeological and historical sites that are located on the Refuge.

seasonal needs of wildlife populations. Grassland management includes establishing and maintaining native prairie areas to provide nesting habitat for waterfowl and other ground nesting bird species. Woodland management involves restoring and enhancing large contiguous blocks of native tree and shrub species for the benefit of neotropical migratory birds, cavity nesting birds, and resident wildlife. Fragmentation has been shown to negatively affect certain wildlife species, for example, the veery and grasshopper sparrow, that require large, relatively continuous blocks of habitat. These species are considered habitat interior species, that is, they favor the interior of the forest (veery) or grassland (grasshopper sparrow) and mostly avoid edges. They are also considered to be area-sensitive, or area-dependent, requiring larger rather than smaller blocks of habitat to meet their breeding and post-breeding needs. As the Refuge implements these management principles, we expect a greater diversity of plant and animal species.

The Refuge contains 82 known wetland basins. Many of the basins have been drained or altered in the past. Of the original grasslands, 99 percent have been altered. Restoration of these wetland basins and grasslands will provide excellent waterfowl production. Throughout the Prairie Pothole Region of Minnesota, an estimated 90 percent of all wetlands and 99 percent of all tallgrass prairie habitat have been lost to development. Many wetland-dependent wildlife species, including waterfowl, have experienced significant long-term population declines due to the continued loss of wetland and grassland habitat in Minnesota, the Dakotas, and prairie Canada. Managing the Refuge wetlands and uplands for waterfowl production and maintenance will contribute toward the habitat and waterfowl production goals identified in the North American Waterfowl Management Plan.

The species of birds that we expect to benefit through habitat management are displayed in a table in Appendix F.

1.0   Habitat Restoration and Wildlife Management Goal:

Restore, preserve and enhance the natural wildlife and plant species diversity within a refuge that is located in the transition zone between the northern tallgrass prairie and the northern hardwood deciduous forest. (See Figure 6, Planned Habitat Restoration and Management, and Table 1, Habitat Conversion.)

As we manage, restore and enhance habitat within the Refuge boundaries, we will evaluate inholdings and surrounding lands for suitable wildlife habitat. We will seek to protect these lands, if appropriate. If it is desirable to acquire the lands, the land will only be acquired from willing sellers.

1.1   Objective: Restore up to 300 acres (10 acres per year) of mesic deciduous forest with emphasis on expanding remnant stands for the benefit of forest interior bird species.

Supplement. Ferio, Svedarsky, and Narog (1999) identified breeding pairs of the following area-sensitive species in the maple-basswood stands on Rydell NWR – red-eyed vireo, ovenbird, great crested flycatcher, rose-breasted grosbeak, veery, pileated woodpecker, American crow, hairy woodpecker. These species, and others, are expected to benefit from forest restoration under this objective.

Figure 5: Planned Habitat Restoration and Management

Legend:
- Wetlands and Wet Meadows
- Grassland/Wetland Complex
- Grass/Shrub Complex
- Maple, Basswood and Oak Forest
- Agricultural Fields
- Conifer Demonstration
- Facilities/Development

0   0.5   1   Miles

Table 1: Habitat Conversion

Planned Habitat Acres

Current Habitat Acres		Lakes	Wetlands and Wet Meadows	Grassland/ Wetland Complex	Grass/Shrub Complex	Maple, Basswood and Oak Forest	Agricultural Fields	Conifer Demonstration	Facilities Development
Lakes	232	232							
Wetlands	338		188	39	28	88			
Hardwood	419		9	15	26	365			
Conifer Plantations	135		3	25	16	86		5	
Grass Meadows	489		12	220	88	163		4	
Cropland	272			115		116	42		
Facilities/ Development	26								26
Grassland/ Wetland Complex	85		24	11	33	17			
Grass/Shrub Complex	11		2	3		6			
Total Acres	**2,007***	**232**	**238**	**428**	**191**	**841**	**42**	**9**	**26**

* Total acres do not equate total legal acreage (2,120) due to lack of precision of GIS at the scale digitized.

Strategies:

1.1.1   Develop a habitat management plan for the Refuge.

1.1.2   Plant native hardwoods and shrubs adjacent to existing woodlands, including planting tamarack trees around Tamarack Lake (to be specified in the Habitat Management Plan).

1.1.3   Phase out mature conifer plantations. Replace/interplant native hardwoods and shrubs into conifer plantations. Manage existing forest stands for native wildlife species.

1.1.4   With partner groups, plant hardwood trees and shrubs. Groups might include the Boy Scouts of America, the Girl Scouts of America, 4-H clubs, Ruffed Grouse Society, Future Farmers of America (FFA) clubs, volunteers, conservation organizations, Friends of the Rydell Refuge, school groups, and garden clubs.

1.1.5   Through the use of fire and other techniques, control invading brush species such as prickly ash and buckthorn in existing woodlands.

1.1.6   In partnership with the University of Minnesota-Crookston, continue the forest health research on the Refuge woodlands.

1.1.7   Clean up 12 abandoned building sites and convert to wildlife habitat. (98013)

1.2 Objective: Restore all of the drained seasonal wetlands by 2003, manage wetland water levels, and re-establish natural hydrologic patterns to benefit waterfowl, fish and other wildlife. (See Figure 6, Planned Water Management.)

Strategies:

1.2.1   Restore drained wetlands to promote waterfowl production and enhance water quality. (00008)

1.2.2   Manage water levels in Sunset, Golden, Swan, and other lakes for waterfowl brood habitat. Manage the water level in Clifford Lake to mimic the natural hydrologic cycle.

1.2.3   Introduce wild rice and wild celery into Church, Otter, and High lakes.

1.2.4   Manage water levels in Swan Lake to provide trumpeter swan nesting habitat.

1.2.5.   Remove minnows from Otter, High, and Church lakes to foster benthic production for the benefit of waterfowl. Construct fish barriers in drainage ditches leaving lakes to restrict minnow reintroduction into the wetlands. (99001)

1.3 Objective: Establish and maintain with fire 300 acres of native prairie grassland to benefit waterfowl, other migratory birds and resident wildlife.

Strategies:

1.3.1   Restore 20 to 50 acres of cropland into native prairie habitat per year. Seed with locally harvested native grasses and prairie forbs.

Figure 6: Planned Water Management

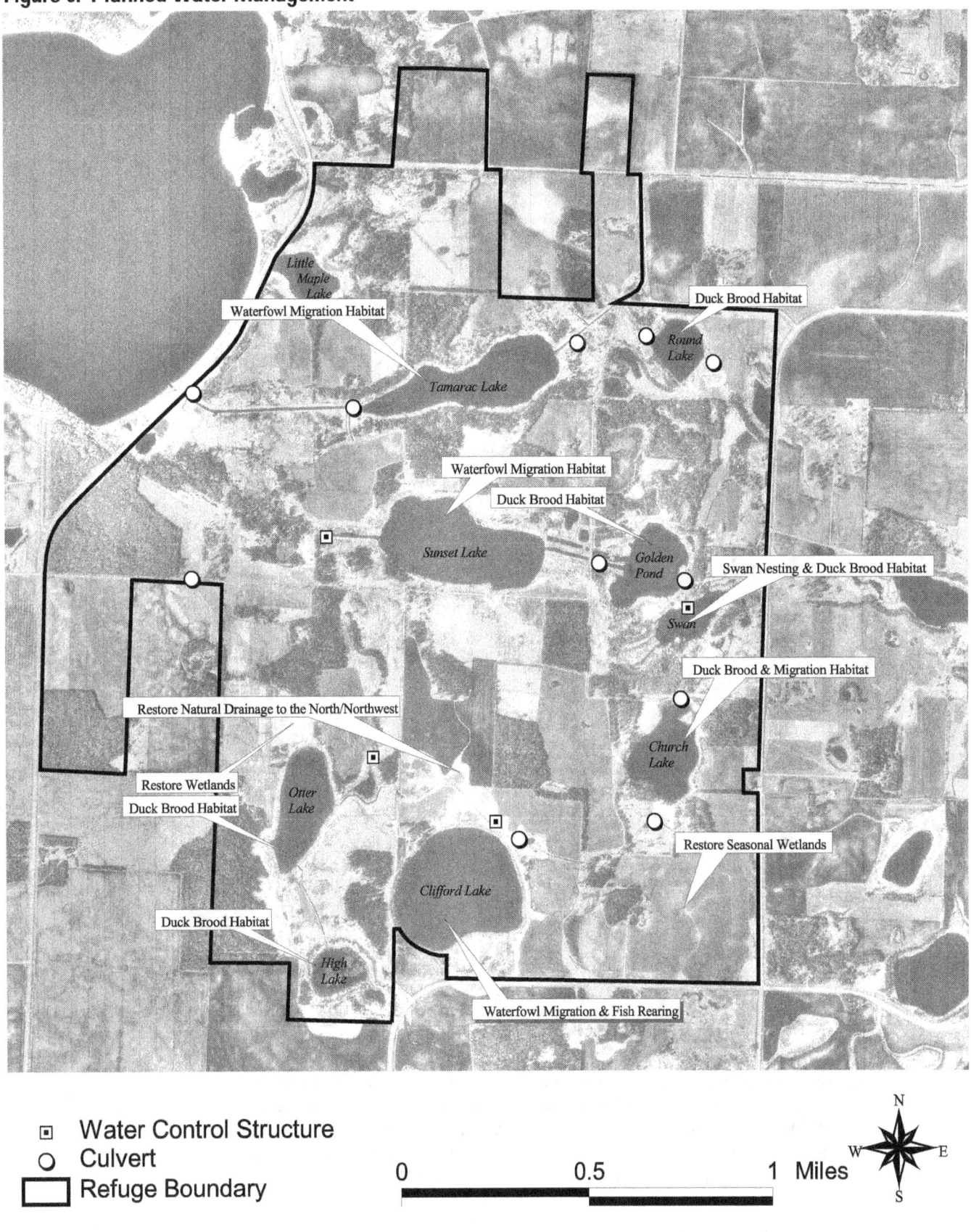

Little Maple Lake

Waterfowl Migration Habitat

Duck Brood Habitat

Round Lake

Tamarac Lake

Waterfowl Migration Habitat

Duck Brood Habitat

Sunset Lake

Golden Pond

Swan Nesting & Duck Brood Habitat

Swan

Duck Brood & Migration Habitat

Church Lake

Restore Natural Drainage to the North/Northwest

Restore Wetlands

Duck Brood Habitat

Otter Lake

Restore Seasonal Wetlands

Duck Brood Habitat

Clifford Lake

High Lake

Waterfowl Migration & Fish Rearing

▣ Water Control Structure
○ Culvert
▭ Refuge Boundary

0   0.5   1 Miles

N
W E
S

The seeding mix should contain at least 50 native grass and forb species. Monitor restored prairie areas for wildlife use. (00017) (00005) (98006)

1.3.2 Enlist partners to assist with grassland establishment and maintenance, i.e. hand stripping forb and grass seeds , hand pulling exotic weeds, and broadcast seeding of new upland areas.

1.3.3 Develop prescription fire plans and a monitoring program for all burn units to facilitate site maintenance and seed production. Burn grassland units on at least a 4-year cycle for maintenance and a 1-year cycle for seed production.

1.3.4 Construct a secure and heated chemical storage shed for chemicals needed in upland restoration work (98001)

1.3.5 Limit the use of chemical sprays for controlling exotic weed species. Primarily use prescribed burning, mowing, biological controls, and hand pulling to control weeds.

1.4 Objective: Using wildlife-compatible farming practices, farm approximately 40 acres of land with no-till farming practices to enhance wildlife viewing opportunities.

Strategy:
1.4.1 Work with University of Minnesota-Crookston to develop a farming program that is both farmer-friendly and that benefits wildlife. Employ a variety of techniques, including no-till/reduced-till/spring-till, buffer strips, contour, residual, and other conservation farming practices to demonstrate benefits for wildlife and provide enhanced opportunities for wildlife viewing. (00014)

1.5 Objective: Promote production of cavity nesting migratory bird species (wood duck, hooded merganser) by protecting all large tree snags and maintaining artificial nesting structures.

Strategy:
1.5.1 Produce wood ducks, hooded mergansers and bluebirds through natural and artificial nesting structures. Enlist partners to build and maintain wood ducks and bluebird nesting structures. (98009)

1.6 Objective: Rear walleye fingerlings to support restoration of native fish to tribal and refuge lands.

Discussion: We are concerned that using the lake for rearing walleye compromises invertebrate and plant production and thus wetland productivity for waterfowl and other migrant water birds. However, because walleye rearing has met the needs of DeSoto and other national wildlife refuges and various Native American tribes, we plan to continue the program while monitoring its effects. We will continue to evaluate the need for rearing walleye in support of restoration of native fish on tribal and refuge lands. If the need is filled, we will discontinue rearing fingerlings. In addition, beginning in the spring of 2002, we will investigate the possible negative impact on invertebrate production and natural wetland productivity in terms of waterfowl and other bird and wildlife use. Our intent is to have a complete assessment of impacts completed by 2005. We will continue rearing walleye until the monitoring shows a negative impact or the needs are met.

Strategy:
1.6.1   With partners, evaluate the need for rearing walleye fingerlings and the effects of rearing walleye on invertebrate production and waterfowl and other wildlife use.

1.7   Objective: Maintain the health and integrity of Sundew Bog.

Strategies:
1.7.1   Maintain the water level in the bog area.

1.7.2   Install an observation boardwalk to facilitate research activities and public education.

1.8   Objective: Determine the abundance and distribution of the Refuge's vascular plants and vertebrates by 2006.

Strategies:
1.8.1   Gather baseline biological data for the Refuge. (98010)

1.8.2   Develop Geographic Information System for the Refuge that includes biological and physical data. (00009)

1.9 Objective: Maintain summer white-tailed deer population at 25 to 30 deer per square mile.

Discussion: If we are to restore woodland habitats, we will need to manage the deer herd to keep it within the limits of the available resources. Deer herd populations can fluctuate significantly with changes in weather conditions, hunting pressure, and food availability. The deer herd can also be affected by the presence of large predators such as wolf, bear, and coyote. All of these factors must be evaluated when determining the appropriate harvest activities. The goal is to have no more than 60 breeding deer on the Refuge after the harvest.

Strategies:
1.9.1   Assess the current herd status each spring to determine harvest strategies for the fall.

1.9.2   Acquire necessary permits from the State of Minnesota to facilitate any needed harvest.

1.9.3   Promote hunts for youth and people with disabilities whenever possible. Allow limited archery and black powder hunts when needed to reduce the breeding population.

Potential Climate Change

The U.S. Department of the Interior issued an order in January 2001 requiring federal agencies under its direction that have land management responsibilities to consider potential climate change impacts as part of long range planning endeavors.

The increase of carbon within the earth's atmosphere has been linked to the gradual rise in surface temperature commonly referred to as global warming. In relation to comprehensive conservation planning for national wildlife refuges, carbon sequestration constitutes the primary climate-related impact to be considered in planning. The U.S. Department of Energy's "*Carbon Sequestration Research and Development*" (U.S. DOE, 1999) defines carbon sequestration as "...the capture and secure storage of carbon that would otherwise be emitted to or remain in the atmosphere."

The land is a tremendous force in carbon sequestration. Terrestrial biomes of all sorts – grasslands, forests, wetlands, tundra, perpetual ice and desert – are effective both in preventing carbon emission and acting as a biological "scrubber" of atmospheric carbon monoxide. The Department of Energy report's conclusions noted that ecosystem protection is important to carbon sequestration and may reduce or prevent loss of carbon currently stored in the terrestrial biosphere.

Preserving natural habitat for wildlife is the heart of any long range plan for national wildlife refuges. The actions proposed in this comprehensive conservation plan would preserve or restore land and water, and would thus enhance carbon sequestration. This in turn contributes positively to efforts to mitigate human-induced global climate changes.

Water Quality Management

The quality of wetland habitat on the Refuge and in Maple Lake is largely determined by the farming practices within the Red Lake Watershed District. In cooperation and partnership with the Red Lake Watershed District and the Maple Lake Improvement Association, the Refuge will take an active role in addressing water quality issues that originate outside of the Refuge boundary. Most activities will be through partnerships with landowners in the watershed, farm and conservation organizations, and appropriate Federal, state, and county agencies.

Refuge staff will work with private landowners, conservation organizations, and governmental agencies to bring programs into the watershed to help meet the water quality goal. Special emphasis will be given to involving landowners along Polk County Ditch 73 in programs and practices such as filter strips, grass waterways, and wetland restoration. The purpose of the program is to reduce the amount of chemical-laden water that flows into the ditch. The program would be designed to give landowners voluntary opportunities to manage their land in a way that improves water quality and benefits wildlife.

This initiative recognizes that agriculture will always be a predominant land use within the watershed. However, it seeks to promote the concept that profitable, sustainable agriculture can be compatible with good water quality and with abundant and diverse wildlife populations.

2.0 Water Quality Management Goal:

With watershed partners, improve and maintain water quality in Rydell National Wildlife Refuge lakes and wetlands and contribute to water quality improvements in Maple Lake. (See Figure 7, Planned Water Quality Management.)

Figure 7: Planned Water Quality Management

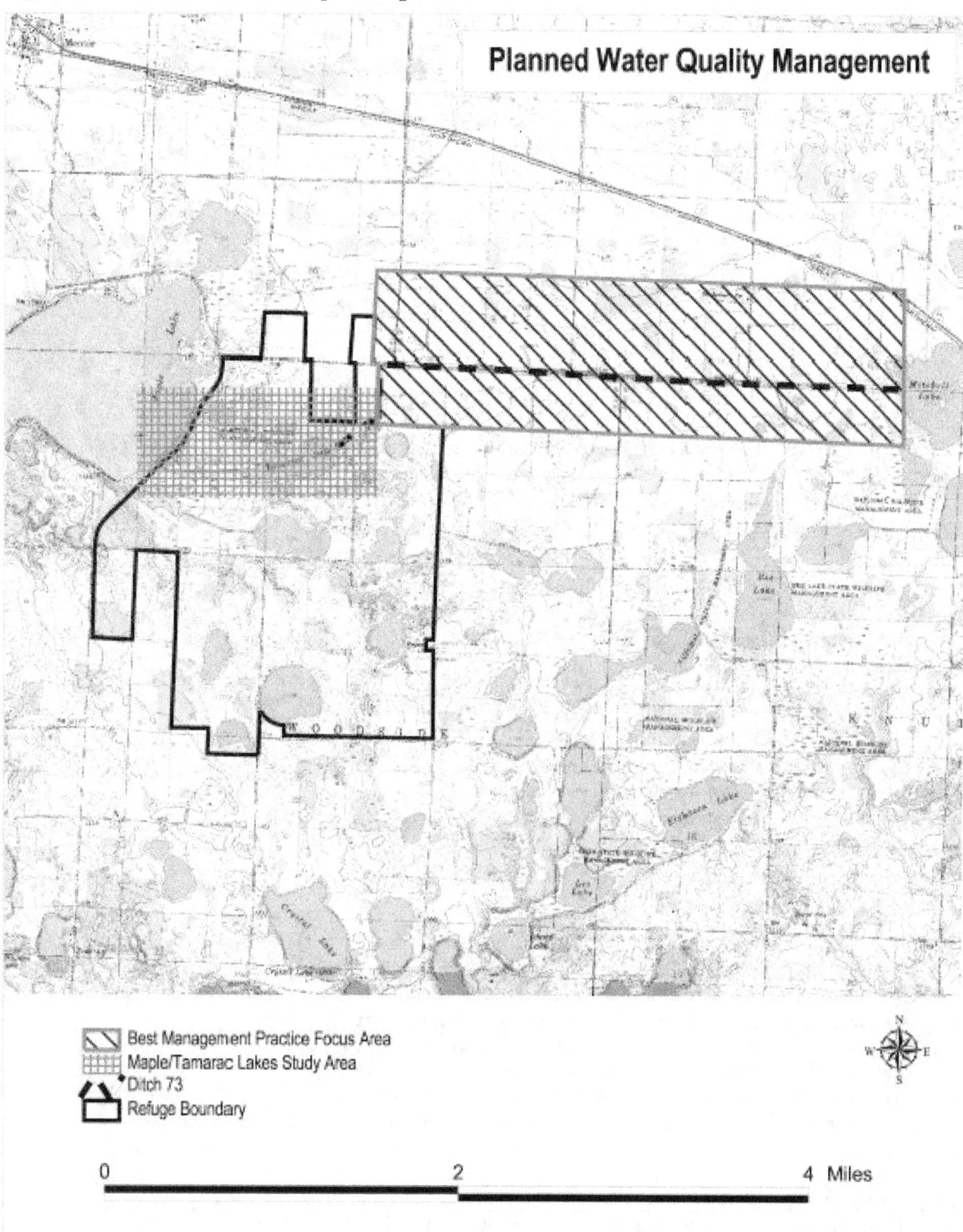

Planned Water Quality Management

- Best Management Practice Focus Area
- Maple/Tamarac Lakes Study Area
- Ditch 73
- Refuge Boundary

0   2   4 Miles

2.1 Objective: Reduce and monitor the phosphorous and nitrate loads that enter the Refuge from Polk County Ditch 73.

Strategies:

2.1.1 Develop a detailed water quality management plan for the Refuge.

2.1.2 Working through the Partners for Fish and Wildlife Program, work with landowners along Ditch 73 to restore drained wetlands and establish grass waterways and buffer zones to slow down and filter the chemical-laden water that flows into the ditch. Establish partnerships with the Maple Lake Improvement Association and other organizations to help cover the costs.

2.1.3 Develop a monitoring system that will effectively determine the nutrient levels that are flowing through and from the Refuge. (00007)

2.1.4 In partnership with the Maple Lake Improvement Association, study the feasibility of slowing down or rerouting the water that is flowing out of Tamarack Lake into Maple Lake. If feasible, develop a plan and secure partners to help complete the project.

Community Involvement

Since it was established in 1992, Rydell National Wildlife Refuge has enjoyed a great deal of public support from people and organizations in the surrounding communities. Community ownership in the Refuge has enabled it to function effectively in an era of budget shortages and minimal staff. Many of the activities presently occurring on the Refuge are only possible because of the large number of dedicated volunteers who are willing to invest their time and energy into the Refuge. Community involvement in Refuge programs will continue to be promoted and encouraged to build an ever increasing base of support. Refuge staff will recruit a cadre of volunteers from the surrounding communities. The volunteers will be trained, equipped, and enabled to become actively involved in many aspects of Refuge management.

The Refuge has formalized a partnership with the Friends of the Rydell Refuge Association. This association will assist the Refuge by seeking funding and providing assistance with the public use and educational programs. A variety of organizations, including the Agassiz Environmental Learning Center, Options Resource Center For Independent Living, the University of Minnesota-Crookston, the Fertile Conservation Club, the Minnesota Deer Hunters Association, the Ruffed Grouse Society and others, have been active in Refuge projects but have not formalized partnership agreements with the Refuge.

3.0 Community Involvement Goal:

Promote community stewardship of the Rydell National Wildlife Refuge through innovative citizen participation in Refuge operations.

3.1 Objective: Establish a self-managed volunteer program that is fully integrated in Refuge operations.

Strategies:

3.1.1 Develop a detailed community involvement plan for the Refuge.

3.1.2 Establish a cost share approach with Friends of the Rydell Refuge to support a volunteer coordinator.

3.1.3 Assist Friends of the Rydell Refuge with technical advice during the preparation of a business management plan.

3.2 Objective: Formalize an educational partnership with Agassiz Environmental Learning Center in Fertile, Minnesota.

Strategy:

3.2.1 Establish a partnership with the Agassiz Environmental Learning Center to develop and present educational programs, activities, and exhibits on the Refuge that promote awareness of wildlife and other natural resources.

3.3 Objective: Formalize an accessibility partnership with Options Resource Center for Independent Living, an East Grand Forks, Minnesota, organization.

Strategy:

3.3.1 Establish a partnership with Options Resource Center for Independent Living to offer hunting, recreation and education programs to special-needs populations.

3.4 Objective: Formalize a research partnership with the University of Minnesota-Crookston.

Strategy:

3.4.1 Establish a partnership with the University of Minnesota-Crookston to use Refuge facilities and environments for off-campus training and, in return, provide continuing research and monitoring of Refuge natural resources.

Public Use

Rydell National Wildlife Refuge currently provides wildlife-oriented recreational opportunities including bird watching, wildlife observation, photography, environmental education, nature programs, deer hunting, hiking and cross country skiing. The Refuge also allows natural resources research activities. Visitation surpassed 5,000 visits in 2000. Maintenance of facilities is largely supported by dedicated volunteers.

Six priority visitor uses are planned for the Rydell National Wildlife Refuge – wildlife observation, photography, environmental education, interpretation, fishing, and hunting. These activities are encouraged within the U.S. Fish & Wildlife Service Refuge System when such activities are compatible with Refuge purposes.

Activities and facilities have been located to minimize conflicts with wildlife and to provide opportunities for solitude and wildlife observation. Approximately 3.5 miles of existing roads and 7 miles of existing trails have been identified for visitor use. These will need to be upgraded so that they are fully accessible and able to withstand increased use. Other roads and trails within the Refuge will be closed to the public and used for maintenance access. Visitor activities will be concentrated in the north central and east central portions of the Refuge, leaving much of the south and west parts of the refuge to function as wildlife sanctuary.

Programs for visitors will promote the enjoyment of the outdoors and a greater understanding and appreciation for fish and wildlife, wildlands ecology, and wildlife management. Specific planning, implementing, and evaluating of the Refuge's public use program will be guided by a step-down Public Use Plan that will be developed following the Comprehensive Conservation Plan. All public use activities must meet the compatibility criteria established for national wildlife refuges before they will be permitted on the Refuge. Activities, uses, and facilities will be phased in over the 15-year time frame as funding and staff become available.

4.0 Public Use Goal:

Provide fully accessible wildlife-dependent recreational opportunities that educate and demonstrate wildlife and habitat stewardship. (See Figure 8, Planned Visitor Facilities.)

4.1 Objective: Meet the needs of 5,000 to 7,000 people per year by improving programs, facilities, and information.

Strategies:

4.1.1 Develop a detailed Public Use Plan that includes appropriate signing, informational brochures, Visitor Center displays, and other information needed to enable visitors to have an educational and enjoyable experience while on the Refuge. (98007) (00002) (98008) (00016)

4.1.2 In partnership with the Friends of the Rydell Refuge, staff the Visitor Center to the extent that the Refuge can be open to the public 6 days per week with an emphasis on evening hours.

4.1.3 In partnership with Options Resource Center for Independent Living and Friends of the Rydell Refuge, make the Visitor Center and headquarters office building and observation decks fully accessible. (00010)

4.2 Objective: Provide visitors with opportunities for wildlife observation, environmental education, interpretation, photography and deer hunting with a strong emphasis on making these activities and facilities fully accessible.

Strategies:

4.2.1 With partners, plan and host two annual "Open House" events at the Refuge. Invite visitors to hike, ski, observe wildlife, tour the Refuge, and learn about the cultural history of the Refuge.

4.2.2 With partners and volunteers, provide deer and waterfowl hunting opportunities for youth and disabled hunters; participate in the

Figure 8: Planned Visitor Facilities

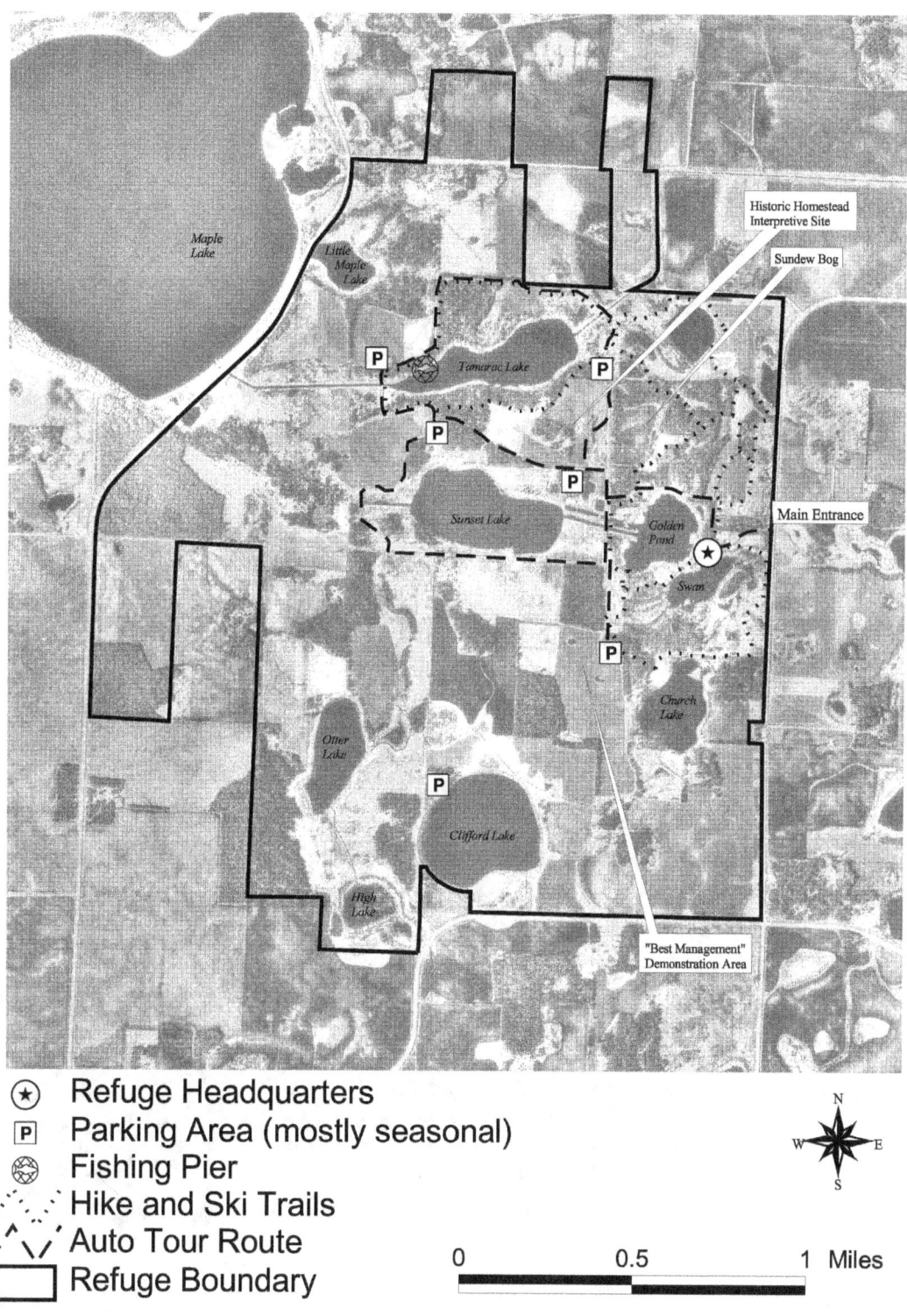

Refuge Headquarters
Parking Area (mostly seasonal)
Fishing Pier
Hike and Ski Trails
Auto Tour Route
Refuge Boundary

0   0.5   1 Miles

Conservation Youth Tours; and present one environmental education workshop each year for local school teachers.

4.2.3 As part of the restoration of Sundew Bog, construct a board walk over the bog to provide access for educational programs. (00010)

4.3 Objective: Establish and maintain a 3.5-mile self-guided interpretive auto tour route for wildlife observation, interpretation and demonstration. Demonstrate effective fish and wildlife management, and soil and water stewardship along the auto tour route.

Strategies:
4.3.1 In partnership with the Polk County Historical Society and the Friends of the Rydell Refuge, identify two or three culturally significant sites to interpret and to enhance visitors' appreciation for the Refuge's cultural history. (00016)

4.3.2 Upgrade the auto tour route so it will be accessible by cars and buses during the spring, summer, and fall months. Include two fully accessible wildlife observation structures at strategic locations along the route. Each observation site will need a parking lot that is large enough to accommodate buses. (00004)

4.4 Objective: Establish and maintain a 7-mile network of accessible trails for wildlife observation, interpretation, and recreational enjoyment.

Strategy:
4.4.1 Develop exhibits and interpretive information for all trails and fishing piers. (00001)

4.5 Objective: Provide high quality fishing opportunities in Tamarack Lake.

Strategies:
4.5.1 Complete a fishing plan and amend refuge-specific regulations to allow fishing on the Refuge.

4.5.2 Complete a fishing pier and access at Tamarack Lake.

4.6 Objective: Promote the "Watchable Wildlife" program and provide accessible facilities for viewing wildlife on the Refuge.

Strategy:
4.6.1 Promote the Refuge as a "Watchable Wildlife" destination. With partner organizations, conduct one watchable wildlife skills workshop per year to educate Refuge visitors on species identification, habitat recognition and wildlife observation skills. Also develop a system of signs, brochures, wildlife identification materials and equipment to provide visitors with enhanced ability to see wildlife.

<u>5.0 Protection Goal:</u>

To protect the biological and cultural integrity of Refuge resources and the health and safety of visitors and Refuge staff.

5.1 Objective: A safe and sanitary environment for visitors and staff.

Strategies:

5.1.1   Construct restroom facilities at the visitor center.

5.1.2   Construct a fuel and chemical storage building.

5.2 Objective: On the average, provide 8 hours per week of field law enforcement.

Strategy:

5.2.1   Hire a resource specialist with law enforcement authority. (00006)

5.3 Objective: Eliminate known electrical line hazard to waterfowl and other birds.

Strategy:

5.3.1   Remove and relocate electrical power lines underground. (00012)

5.4 Objective: Staff and operate the Refuge to achieve minimum standards of protection to the resource and service to the public.

Strategies:

5.4.1   Provide basic facilities and maintenance for the Refuge. (00011)

5.4.2   Provide basic office equipment and administrative support for the staff. (00003)(98012)

5.5 Objective: Fulfill requirements of Section 14 of the Archaeological Resources Protection Act and Section 110 (a) (2) of the National Historic Preservation Act.

Strategy:

5.5.1   Establish a plan that will meet the requirements of the Archaeological Resources Protection Act for surveying lands to identify archaeological resources and the National Historic Preservation Act for a preservation program.

Chapter 5: Plan Implementation

Partnerships

The future of Rydell National Wildlife Refuge, like most national wildlife refuges, is dependent upon a public constituency that is aware of Refuge and environmental issues and that is willing to work toward resolving them. The expanded educational, recreational, and partnership opportunities proposed by this CCP will help build and maintain this constituency. Promoting the Refuge as a natural and recreational asset in northwestern Minnesota will enhance the Refuge's image and help build public support.

A key component in implementing the CCP will be the development of partnerships with organizations, agencies, and individuals. Partnership potential exists with institutions and organizations that include:

- University of Minnesota-Crookston
- Friends of the Rydell Refuge
- Agassiz Environmental Learning Center
- Local school districts
- Maple Lake Improvement Association
- Options Resource Center for Independent Living
- Polk County Park Board
- East Polk County Soil and Water Conservation District
- Minnesota Department of Natural Resources
- Advanced Hunter Education Program
- Fertile Conservation Club
- Minnesota Deer Hunters Association
- Numerous individual volunteers
- Ruffed Grouse Society
- Minnesota Waterfowl Association
- Ducks Unlimited

The refuge manager will seek to establish partnerships with these and other organizations or agencies that have an interest in working together to benefit wildlife, the Refuge, and their communities.

Personnel Needs

Figure 9: Current Staffing

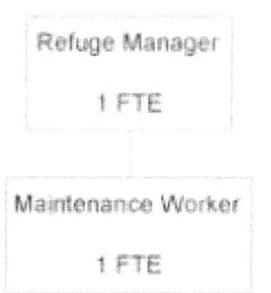

A manager and a maintenance worker are assigned to the Refuge operations (see Figure 9). Eventually, as many as five staff members, including a park ranger, biological technician, and clerk, will be stationed at the Refuge to implement the goals and objectives identified in this CCP (see Figure 10). In addition, a paid position for a volunteer coordinator is expected to be funded through a cost share partnership with the Friends of the Rydell Refuge Association. Annual Work Plans will reflect the priorities and intent of the long-range CCP. When discretionary funding and staff time is available, it will be used to implement additional components of the plan.

Step-down Management Plans

The CCP provides broad conceptual guidance for future protection, management, and development of the Rydell National Wildlife Refuge. Before the projects are implemented, additional detailed plans will need to be prepared. Refuge staff will continue to look for innovative partnerships with local professionals and businesses to help with preparing the plans.

Several step-down management plans must be completed to better describe the planned work and to meet Service policy. Within the next 4 years the following plans will be completed:

- Inventory and Monitoring
- Habitat Monitoring
- Public Use
- Law Enforcement
- Cultural Resource Management
- Hunt Management
- Fire Management
- Cropland Management
- Fisheries Management
- Forest Management

Figure 10: Proposed Organization Chart

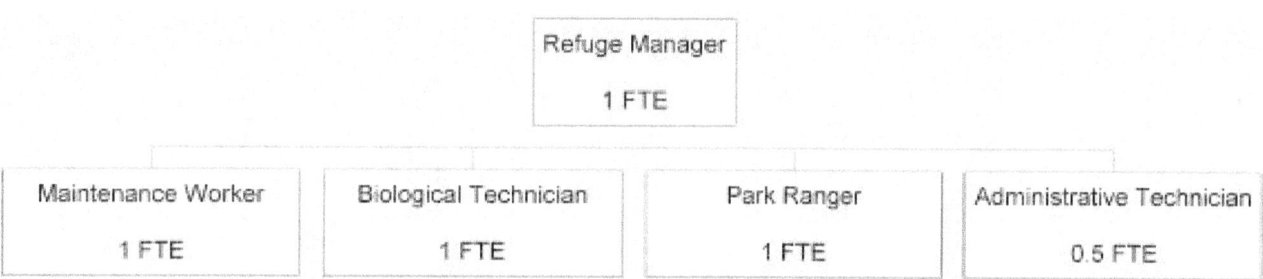

Funding

Funding will come through a variety of internal and external sources. Refuge Maintenance funds will be used to renovate some of the facilities identified in this plan. However, these funds are in short supply, and Refuge staff will look for ways of leveraging and matching dollars through new and innovative public and private sources. The full implementation of this plan will be dependent on new sources of funding as a result of partnerships and grants.

The Friends of the Rydell Refuge Association will be an important means of connecting the Refuge with interested local citizens and organizations that are willing and able to contribute time and money to the development of the programs identified in this plan. Volunteers will also play a critical role in assisting Refuge staff with fulfilling the future vision of Rydell National Wildlife Refuge.

Monitoring and Evaluation

Monitoring is critical to successful implementation of this plan. Monitoring is necessary to evaluate the progress toward objectives and to determine if conditions are changing. The techniques and details for monitoring related to specific objectives will be specified in the Inventory and Monitoring Step-down Plan.

Every 5 years this plan will be revisited to document progress, reassess its direction and determine if any modifications are necessary to meet changing conditions. Public involvement in evaluating progress and plan implementation will be encouraged. Increased public visitation and new facilities will be evaluated for compatibility with Refuge purposes.

Index

A

Agassiz Environmental Learning Center 5, 32, 33, 38
Agriculture 7, 10, 12, 13, 28, 30

B

Bird Conservation Areas 10
Birds 23, 28, 37
  migratory birds 1, 2, 3, 9, 10, 21, 23, 26

C

Clifford Lake 19
Community Involvement 7, 21, 32, 33
Comprehensive Conservation Plan 1, 2, 6, 34
County Ditch 73 7, 30, 32
Cropland Management 19, 26, 28
Cultural Resources 6, 16, 34, 36, 37

D

Detroit Lakes Wetland Management District 11, 17

E

East Polk County 19
East Polk County SWCD 5, 19, 38
Endangered Species 2, 3, 9, 11
Environmental Assessment, Rydell NWR 3, 6
Environmental Education 1, 21, 32, 33, 34, 36, 38
Erskine 12
Exotic Species 8, 28

F

Fertile Conservation Club 38
Fish 1, 2, 3, 7, 9, 21, 26, 28, 34, 91, 96, 101, 103, 105, 107
  Fish Management 1, 3, 6, 19, 36
Fish and Wildlife Act of 1956 3, 91, 93, 96, 99, 101, 103, 105, 107
Fish Hatchery, Rydell NWR 3, 7, 16
Friends of the Rydell Refuge Association 5, 17, 26, 32, 33, 34, 36, 38, 39, 40
Funding, Rydell NWR 2

G

Grassland 8, 9, 10, 11, 13, 19, 21, 23, 26, 28
Grove Park Township 12

H

Habitat Restoration 1, 10, 11, 21, 23, 26

I

Invasive Species 13

L

Location and size, Rydell NWR 1

M

Maple Lake 7, 30, 32
Maple Lake Improvement District 5, 18, 32, 38
Mellon Foundation 1, 5, 12, 21
Mentor 12
Minnesota Deer Hunters Association 32, 38
Minnesota Department of Natural Resources 5, 7, 18, 19, 38

N

National Wildlife Refuge Improvement Act 1
National Wildlife Refuge System 2, 11, 12
North American Waterfowl Management Plan 3, 23

O

Options Resource Center for Independent Living 18, 33, 38

P

Partners in Flight 10
Partnerships 1, 2, 5, 11, 26, 28, 29, 30, 32, 33, 34, 36, 38, 39
Polk County 1, 12, 38
Polk County Historical Society 36
Prescribed Fire 26, 28
Public Use 1, 2, 5, 7, 17, 18, 21, 28, 32, 33, 34, 36

S

Sundew Bog 8, 13, 36

T

Threatened Species 2, 9, 11, 16

U

U.S. Fish & Wildlife Service
      1, 2, 3, 5, 6, 9, 10, 11, 12, 16, 19, 21, 33, 91, 93, 96, 99, 101, 103, 105, 107
U.S. Prairie Pothole Joint Venture 11
Union Lake Sarah Improvement Association 5
University of Minnesota-Crookston 13, 26, 28, 32, 33, 38
Uplands 1, 11, 23, 28

V

Vision, Rydell National Wildlife Refuge 1
Volunteers 7, 17, 18, 19, 26, 32, 33, 34

W

Water 1, 3, 6, 7, 21, 26, 32, 36
  Water Quality 7, 26, 30, 32
Waterfowl 1, 7, 9, 10, 11, 12, 16, 21, 23, 26, 28, 37
Waterfowl Production Area 2, 3, 11, 12
Wetland Management Districts 2
Wetlands 1, 7, 8, 9, 10, 11, 16, 19, 21, 23, 26, 30, 32
Wildlife
    1, 2, 3, 9, 10, 11, 16, 17, 18, 21, 23, 26, 28, 30, 33, 34, 36, 103, 105, 107
  Wildlife Management 1, 3, 10, 13, 18, 21, 23, 34, 36
Wildlife-dependent Recreation 1, 5, 21, 34, 36
Woodlands 1, 9, 12, 17, 21, 26
Woodside Township 12

Appendix

Appendix A: Glossary

Appendix B: Bibliography

Appendix C: Chronology of Events at Rydell National Wildlife Refuge

Appendix D: Library Distribution

Appendix E: Project List

Appendix F: Species List

Appendix G: Compliance Requirements

Appendix H: Compatibility Determinations

Appendix I: Environmental Assessment

Appendix J: Mailing List

Appendix K: List of Preparers

Appendix L: Summary and Disposition of Public Comments Received on the Draft CCP

Appendix A: Glossary

Appendix A: Glossary

Alternative:	A set of objectives and strategies needed to achieve refuge goals and the desired future condition.
Biological Diversity:	The variety of life forms and its processes, including the variety of living organisms, the genetic differences among them, and the communities and ecosystems in which they occur.
Compatible Use:	A wildlife-dependent recreational use, or any other use on a refuge that will not materially interfere with or detract from the fulfillment of the mission of the Service or the purposes of the refuge.
Comprehensive Conservation Plan:	A document that describes the desired future conditions of the refuge, and specifies management actions to achieve refuge goals and the mission of the National Wildlife Refuge System.
Ecosystem:	A dynamic and interrelated complex of plant and animal communities and their associated non-living environment.
Ecosystem Approach:	A strategy or plan to protect and restore the natural function, structure, and species composition of an ecosystem, recognizing that all components are interrelated.
Ecosystem Management:	Management of an ecosystem that includes all ecological, social and economic components that make up the whole of the system.
Endangered Species:	Any species of plant or animal defined through the Endangered Species Act as being in danger of extinction throughout all or a significant portion of its range, and published in the Federal Register.
Environmental Assessment:	A systematic analysis to determine if proposed actions would result in a significant effect on the quality of the environment.
Goals:	Descriptive statements of desired future conditions.

Issue:	Any unsettled matter that requires a management decision. For example, a resource management problem, concern, a threat to natural resources, a conflict in uses, or in the presence of an undesirable resource condition.
National Wildlife Refuge System:	All lands, waters, and interests therein administered by the U.S. Fish and Wildlife Service as wildlife refuges, wildlife ranges, wildlife management areas, waterfowl production areas, and other areas for the protection and conservation of fish, wildlife and plant resources.
Objectives:	Actions to be accomplished to achieve a desired outcome.
Preferred Alternative:	The Service's selected alternative identified in the Draft Comprehensive Conservation Plan.
Scoping:	A process for determining the scope of issues to be addressed by a comprehensive conservation plan and for identifying the significant issues. Involved in the scoping process are federal, state and local agencies; private organizations; and individuals.
Species:	A distinctive kind of plant or animal having distinguishable characteristics, and that can interbreed and produce young. A category of biological classification.
Strategies:	A general approach or specific actions to achieve objectives.
Threatened Species:	Those plant or animal species likely to become endangered species throughout all of or a significant portion of their range within the foreseeable future. A plant or animal identified and defined in accordance with the 1973 Endangered Species Act and published in the Federal Register.
Vegetation:	Plants in general, or the sum total of the plant life in an area.
Vegetation Type:	A category of land based on potential or existing dominant plan species of a particular area.
Watershed:	The entire land area that collects and drains water into a stream or stream system.

Wetland: Areas such as lakes, marshes, and streams that
                          are inundated by surface or ground water for a
                          long enough period of time each year to support,
                          and that do support under natural conditions,
                          plants and animals that require saturated or
                          seasonally saturated soils.

Wildlife Diversity: A measure of the number of wildlife species in
                          an area and their relative abundance.

Wildlife-dependent
Recreational Use: A use of refuge that involves hunting, fishing,
                          wildlife observation and photography, or envi-
                          ronmental education and interpretation, as
                          identified in the National Wildlife Refuge
                          System Improvement Act of 1997.

Appendix B: Bibliography

Appendix B: Bibliography

Rydell National Wildlife Refuge Environmental Assessment and Preliminary Management Plan. November 1991. U.S. Fish and Wildlife Service

A Vegetative Survey of the Rydell National Wildlife Refuge. P.R. Baird, J.M. Dyer, and W.D. Svedarsky. July 1995

A Cultural Resources Management Plan for the Rydell National Wildlife Refuge. J.A. Ward, J.P. McCarthy. February 1997.

Polk County Comprehensive Local Water Plan, 1996 Revision. N. Hoberg and G. Lee. September 1996.

Maple Lake Citizen Monitoring Project. Maple Lake Assessment Report. W.R. Goeken. December 1992.

Environment; NEPA Handbook -- Introduction (30 AM 2). September 23, 1983. U.S. Fish and Wildlife Service Administrative Manual.

Environment; NEPA Handbook -- Intra-Service Planning and Documentation (30 AM 3). September 23, 1983. U.S. Fish and Wildlife Service Administrative Manual.

Environmental Quality; National Environmental Policy Act; Documenting and Implementing Decisions (550 FW 3). March 29, 1996. U.S. Fish and Wildlife Service Manual.

Ferio, T.A., W.D. Svedarsky, and S.M. Narog. 1999. Breeding birds of remnant maple-basswood stands on the Rydell National Wildlife Refuge, 1998. Final report conducted under contract order n. 32583-8-M009 for the U.S. Fish and Wildlife Service. 11p.

Fish and Wildlife Service (National Environmental Policy Act Implementing Procedures; 516 DM 6, Appendix 1). January 16, 1997. Appendix 1 to U.S. Department of the Interior Manual; Environmental Quality; National Environmental Policy Act of 1969; Managing the NEPA Process (516 DM 6). March 18, 1980

How to Write Quality EISs and EAs; Guidelines for NEPA Documents. 1992. Shipley Associates.

Management and General Public Use of the National Wildlife Refuge System (E.O. 12996). March 25, 1996.

Minnesota Department of Transportation. 1998. Marschner Map of Presettlement Vegetation in Minnesota. Distributor: Chief Archaeologist, Cultural Resource Unit, 395 John Ireland boulevard, Mail Stop 676, St. Paul, MN 55155-1899.

National Environmental Policy Act of 1969 (40 U.S.C. 4321 et seq.).

National Wildlife Refuge System Administration Act of 1966 (16 U.S.C. 668dd-668jj).

Planning; NEPA Compliance (4 RM 5). March 12, 1982. U.S. Fish and Wildlife Service Refuge Manual.

Public Use Requirements Handbook; October 1984, U.S. Fish and Wildlife Service.

Redelegation of Authority - Signatory on Finding of No Significant Impact. July 16, 1996. Region 1 Policy Book - Regional Policy Order No. 96-08.

Refuge Management; Refuge Planning; Policy and Responsibilities (602 FW 1). June 23, 1995. U.S. Fish and Wildlife Service Manual

Refuge Management; Refuge Planning; Planning Process (602 FW 2). November 12, 1996. U.S. Fish and Wildlife Service Manual.

Refuge Management; Refuge Planning; Step-down Management Planning (602 FW 3). June 23, 1995. U.S. Fish and Wildlife Service Manual.

Refuge Recreation Act of 1962 (16 U.S.C. 460k - 460k-4).

Regulations for Implementing the Procedural Provisions of the National Environmental Policy Act (40 CFR 1500-1508). September 23, 1983. President's Council on Environmental Quality.

Writing Refuge Management Goals and Objectives: A Handbook. March 1996. Supplement to 602 FW 1-3 of the U.S. Fish and Wildlife Service Manual.

Appendix C: Chronology of Events

Appendix C: Chronology of Events

Rydell National Wildlife Refuge

1967	The first tract of land was purchased by Leonard Rydell (Ramberg homestead).
1971	The house near the maintenance shop was built.
1972	The main house was built (Headquarters Office).
1974	The township roads were closed through abandonment proceedings.
1985	The fish hatchery construction was completed and walleye rearing began.
1985	Two hundred Canada geese were released on the property.
1986	A pair of mature trumpeter swans were released on the property. Thirty-nine immature swans were kept on the property until they were released at several northern Minnesota sites.
1988	176,000 conifer, hardwood and fruit bearing trees were planted on the property.
1992	The Richard King Mellon Foundation purchased the property and transferred it to the U.S. Fish and Wildlife Service to be managed as a national wildlife refuge.
1992	Bob Hiltner was hired as the first permanent full-time employee of Rydell NWR.
1992	The first Polk County SWCD youth conservation tours were conducted on the Refuge.
1992	The first volunteer began working on the Refuge.
1994	The first deer hunts were conducted on the Refuge to manage the excessive deer population.
1995	Seventeen abandoned wells and three cisterns at old building sites were capped.
1996	The first prescribed burn was conducted on the Refuge.
1996	The Friends of the Rydell Refuge Association was formed and incorporated.

1996	The former pool house was filled to convert the building into a visitor center.
1996	The first open house was held on the Refuge with 290 people attending.
1996	With the help of volunteers, the Refuge Visitor Center first opened to the public.
1996	The first deer hunt for persons with disabilities was conducted on the Refuge.
1996	A youth deer hunting skills training program and youth deer hunt were initiated.
1997	The Minnesota State Legislature provided $200,000 to the Friends of Rydell Refuge Association to make Refuge facilities accessible.
1998	Volunteers began forest restoration with replanting on 20 acres.
2000	Refuge visitation surpassed the 5,000 mark for the first time.

Appendix D: Library Distribution

Appendix D: Library Distribution

Rydell National Wildlife Refuge Draft CCP

Bagley Public Library
21 Main Ave. North
Bagley, MN 56621

East Grand Forks Public Library
223 2nd Avenue Northwest
East Grand Forks, MN 56721

Grand Forks Public Library
2110 Library Circle
Grand Forks, ND 58206

Polk County Library
Fertile Branch
212 Mill Street North
Fertile, MN 56540

Crookston Public Library
110 North Ash
Crookston, MN 56716

Fosston Public Library
405 North Foss
Fosston, MN 56542

McIntosh Public Library
McIntosh, MN 56556

Red Lake Falls Public Library
109 Main Avenue Southwest
Red Lake Falls, MN 56750

Appendix E: Project List

Appendix C: RONS and MMS
Refuge Operation Needs System List (RONS)

RONS Project Cost Summary – Refuge Project Priorities

The projects are prioritized based on the likelihood and potential impact of the project.

RONS No.	Strategy No.	Project Description	First Year Need
98006	1.3.1	Native prairie establishment and maintenance	$114,000
00017	1.3.1	Native prairie establishment and maintenance	$119,000
98012	5.4.2	Increase administrative capabilities	$55,000
00011	5.4.1	Minimum refuge operations needs	$53,000
00012	5.3.1	Remove waterfowl hazard	$76,000
00006	5.2.1	Hire resource specialist with law enforcement	$129,000
99001	2.2.1-4	Restoration of diving duck habitat	$35,000
00005	1.3.1	Harvest of native prairie seed for restoration work	$31,000
98007	4.1.1	Development of education/ interpretation programs	$40,000
98008	4.4.1	Improve visitor accommodations	$82,000
00001	4.4.1	Develop exhibits and interpretive information for trail system	$31,000
00004	4.3.2	Develop watchable wildlife auto tour route	$348,000
98013	1.1.7	Conversion of old home sites to wildlife habitat	$102,000
00008	1.2.1	Restore drained wetland basins	$38,000

RONS No.	Strategy No.	Project Description	First Year Need
00009	1.8.2	Develop geographic information database	$33,000
00010	4.2.3	Construct accessible interpretive bog walk	$61,000
00016	5.1.1	Construct restroom facility for visitors center	$94,000
98001	5.1.2	Construct fuel and chemical storage building	$75,000
98010	1.8.1	Expand biological community identification and numeration	$143,000
00007	2.1.3	Evaluate aquatic resources and water quality	$36,000
00002	4.1.1.	Create audiovisual program for visitor center	$46,000
98009	1.5.1	Promote artificial nest structure program	$20,000
00003	5.4.2	Purchase office furniture	$20,000
00014	1.4.1	Conservation farming demonstration program	$80,000

Appendix F: Species List

Appendix F: Species List

Mammals

Arctic Shrew	*Sorex arcticus*
Masked Shrew	*Sorex cinereus*
Northern Water Shrew	*Sorex palustris*
Pygmy Shrew	*Sorex hoyi*
Shorttail Shrew	*Blarina brevicauda*
Starnose Mole	*Condylura cristata*
Little Brown Myotis	*Myotis lucifugus*
Keen's Myotis	*Myotis keenii*
Silver-haired Bat	*Lasionycteris noctivagans*
Big Brown Bat	*Eptesicus fuscus*
Red Bat	*Lasiurus borealis*
Hoary Bat	*Lasiurus cinereus*
Eastern Cottontail	*Sylvilagus floridanus*
Snowshoe Hare	*Lepus americanus*
Whitetail Jackrabbit	*Lepus townsendii*
Woodchuck	*Marmota monax*
Eastern Fox Squirrel	*Sciurus niger*
Eastern Gray Squirrel	*Sciurus carolinensis*
Red Squirrel	*Tamiasciurus hudsonicus*
Northern Flying Squirrel	*Glaucomys sabrinus*
Thirteen-lined Ground Squirrel	*Spermophilus tridecemlineatus*
Least Chipmunk	*Tamias minimus*
Eastern Chipmunk	*Tamias striatus*
Beaver	*Castor canadensis*
White-footed Mouse	*Peromyscus leucopus*
Deer Mouse	*Peromyscus maniculatus*
Meadow Jumping Mouse	Zapus hudsonius
Boreal Redback Vole	*Clethrionomys gapperi*
Meadow Vole	*Microtus pennsylvanicus*
Prairie Vole	*Microtus ochrogaster*
House Mouse	*Mus musculus*
Plains Pocket Gopher	*Geomys bursarius*
Norway Rat	*Rattus norvegicus*
Muskrat	*Ondatra zibethicus*
Least Weasel	*Mustela nivalis*
Longtail Weasel	*Mustela frenata*
Shorttail weasel	*Mustela erminea*
Mink	*Mustela vison*
River Otter	*Lutra canadensis*
Raccoon	*Procyon lotor*
Striped Skunk	*Mephitis mephitis*
Spotted Skunk	*Spilogale putorius*
Porcupine	*Erethizon dorsatum*

Badger	*Taxidea taxus*
Red fox	*Vulpes vulpes*
Coyote	*Canis latrans*
Gray Wolf	*Canis lupus*
Black Bear	*Ursus americanus*
Bobcat	*Lynx rufus*
Whitetail deer	*Odocoileus virginianus*
Moose	*Alces alces*

Reptiles and Amphibians

Snapping turtle	*Chelydra serpentina*
Western Painted Turtle	*Chrysemys picta belii*
Smooth Green Snake	*Liochlorophis vernalis*
Northern Red-bellied Snake	*Storeria occipitomaculata occipitomaculata*
Plains Garter Snake	*Thamnophis radix*
Red-sided Garter Snake	*Thamnophis sirtalis parietalis*
Northern ribbon snake	*Thamnophis suaritus*
Mudpuppy	*Necturus maculosus*
Eastern Tiger salamander	*Ambystoma tigrinum*
American Toad	*Bufo americanus*
Canadian Toad	*Bufo hemiophrys*
Great Plains Toad	*Bufo cognatus*
Northern Spring Peeper	*Pseudacris crucifer crucifer*
Boreal Chorus Frog	*Pseudacris triseriata*
Gray Treefrog	*Hyla versicolor*
Swamp Tree Frog	*Pseudacris nigrita.*
Wood Frog	*Rana sylvatica*

Butterflies

Dusted Skipper	*Atrytonopsis hianna*
Dun Skipper	*Euphyes vestris*
Delaware Skipper	*Anatrytone logan*
Dakota Skipper	*Hesperia dacotae*
Northern Broken-Dash	*Wallengrenia egeremet*
Peck's Skipper	*Polites peckius*
Tawny-edged Skipper	*Polites themistocles*
Long Dash	*Polites mystic*
Poweshiek Skipperling	*Oarisma poweshiek*
Common Checkered-Skipper	*Pyrgus communis*
Dreamy Duskywing	*Erynnis icelus*
Black Swallowtail	*Papilio polyxenes*
Checkered White	*Pontia protodice*
Cabbage White	*Pieris rapae*
Alfalfa Butterfly	*Colias eurytheme*
Common Sulphur	*Colias philodice*
Purplish Copper	*Lycaena helloides*
Melissa Blue	*Lycaeides melissa*

Viceroy	*Limenitis archippus*
Red Admiral	*Vanessa atalanta*
Painted Lady	*Vanessa cardui*
Mourning Cloak	*Nymphalis antiopa*
Pearl Crescent	*Phyciodes tharos*
Harris' Checkerspot	*Chlosyne harrisii*
Silvery Checkerspot	*Chlosyne nycteis*
Silver-bordered Fritillary	*Pieris rapae*
Regal Fritillary	*Speyeria idalia*
Great Spangled Fritillary	*Speyeria cybele*
Aphrodite Fritillary	*Speyeria aphrodite*
Variegated Fritillary	*Euptoieta claudia*
Monarch Butterfly	*Danaus plexippus*
Eyed Brown	*Satyrodes eurydice*
Inornate Ringlet	*Coenonympha inornata*
Common Wood Nymph	*Cercyonis pegala*

Source for scientific names:

Opler, Paul A., Harry Pavulaan, and Ray E. Stanford (coordinators). 1995. Butterflies of North America. Jamestown, ND: Northern Prairie Wildlife Research Center Home Page. http://www.npwrc.usgs.gov/resource/distr/lepid/bflyusa/bflyusa.htm (Version 17AUG2000).

The following table was compiled from four sources – the Refuge's bird list (first six columns); the January 1999 edition of the Region 3 Fish & Wildlife Resource Conservation Priorities (last column); Minnesota's List of Endangered, Threatened, and Special Concern Species (last column). Leslie Peterson, Biologist for Detroit Lakes Wetland Management District, completed the entries for "Potential Benefit by Habitat Objectives" columns from his professional knowledge, experience, and judgment.

Species (**Bold** indicates species that are abundant or common on the refuge for at least part of the year)	Nested on refuge recently	Status On Refuge				Potential Benefit by Habitat Objectives (Habitat used regularly for **f**ood, **n**esting, or **c**over)				Status In Region and State
		a - abundant: a common species that is very numerous c - common: certain to be seen or heard in suitable habitat, not in large numbers u - uncommon: present, but not always seen o - occasional: seen only a few times during the season r - rare: seen every two to five years				1	2	3	4	R3 - Region 3 Conservation Priority SMC - Species of Mgt. Concern SSC- State Special Concern ST - State Threatened SE - State Endangered T - Federal Threatened E - Federal Endangered
		Spring	Summer	Fall	Winter	Restore mesic deciduous forest 500 acres	Restore and manage wetlands for waterfowl and other wildlife	Establish native prairie grassland 300 acres	Manage cropland for wildlife food and viewing opportunities 40 acres	
Birds With Special Regional Status										
Common Loon	Y	c	c	o			f,c			R3,SMC
Horned Grebe		r		r			f,c			ST
American White Pelican		r	r	r			f,c			SSC
Double-crested Cormorant		o	o	o			f,c			R3
American Bittern		o	o	o			f,c			R3,SMC
Snow Goose		r		r			f,c	c	f	R3
Canada Goose (giant race)	Y	a	a	a	o		f,n,c	c	f	R3
Canada Goose (EPP)		c	o	c			f,c	c	f	R3
Trumpeter Swan	Y	c	c	u			f,n,c			R3,SMC,ST
Wood Duck	Y	c	c	c		f,n,c				R3
American Black Duck		r	r	r			f,c	f,c	f	R3
Mallard	Y	c	c	c	r		f,n,c	f,n,c	f	R3
Blue-winged Teal		u	u	u			f,c	c	f	R3
Northern Pintail		r		r			f,c	c	f	R3
Canvasback		o	r	o			f,c			R3
Lesser Scaup		u	r	u			f,c			R3
Bald Eagle		u	u	u	r	f,n,c	f	f	f	R3,T,SSC
Northern Harrier		u	u	u		n,c	f	f	f	R3, SMC
Northern Goshawk	Y				r	f,c	f	f	f	R3, SMC
Peregrine Falcon		r		r		f,c	f	f	f	R3,E,ST

Species (Bold indicates species that are abundant or common on the refuge for at least part of the year)	Nesting? Y=Yes	Status on Refuge (See top of table for codes)				Potential Benefit f=food, n=nesting, c=cover				Status in Region and State (See top for codes)
		Sp	S	Fall	W	Forest	Wet.	Grass.	Crop	
Upland Sandpiper		o	o	o			f,c			R3, SMC
American Woodcock		o	o	o		f,n,c	f,c			R3
Franklin's Gull		u		u			f,c			SSC
Common Tern		u	o	u			f,c			R3,SMC,ST
Forester's Tern		u	o	u			f,c			SSC
Black Tern		u	o	u			f,c			R3,SMC
Yellow-billed Cuckoo		r	r	r		f,c				R3,SMC
Northern Flicker		u	o	u	r	f,c				R3,SMC
Acadian Flycatcher		r	r	r		f,c				SSC
Sedge Wren	Y	u	c	u			f,n,c			R3,SMC
Veery		o	r	r		f,c				R3,SMC
Chestnut-sided Warbler		u	o	u		f,c				R3,SMC
Field Sparrow		o	o	o		f,c		f,c	f,c	R3,SMC
Grasshopper Sparrow		o		o		f,c		f,c	f,c	R3,SMC
Bobolink	Y	u	c	u			f,c	f,n,c	f,n,c	R3,SMC
Eastern Meadowlark		r	r	r				f,c	f,c	R3,SMC
Birds Currently Not on Regional Lists										
Pied-billed Grebe	Y	u	u	u			f,n,c			
Eared Grebe		r		r			f,c			
Red-necked Grebe		o	o	o			f,c			
Great blue Heron		c	c	u			f,c			
Green Heron		o	o	o			f,c			
Tundra Swan		r		r			f,c			
Green-winged Teal		o	o	o			f,c	c	f,c	
Northern Shoveler		o	r	r			f,c	c		
Gadwall		o		o			f,c	c	f,c	
American Wigeon		o		o			f,c	c	f,c	
Redhead		o	r	o			f,c			
Ring-necked Duck		u	o	u			f,c			
Greater Scaup		r		r			f,c			

Species (**Bold** indicates species that are abundant or common on the refuge for at least part of the year)	Nesting? Y=Yes	Status on Refuge (See top of table for codes)				Potential Benefit f=food, n=nesting, c=cover				Status in Region and State (See top for codes)
		Sp	S	Fall	W	Forest	Wet.	Grass.	Crop	
Common Goldeneye		u	r	u			f,c			
Bufflehead		u	r	u			f,c			
Ruddy Duck		r		r			f,c			
Hooded Merganser	Y	o	o	o		n	f,n,c			
Common Merganser		o		o			f,c			
Red-breasted Merganser		o		0			f,c			
Turkey Vulture		r		r		f,c	f	f	f	
Osprey		r	r	r		f,c	f	f	f	
Sharp-shinned Hawk		o	o	o	r	f,c	f	f	f	
Cooper's Hawk	Y	o	o	o	r	f,n,c	f	f	f	
Red-tailed Hawk	Y	c	c	c		f,n,c	f	f	f	
Rough-legged Hawk		r		r		f,c	f	f	f	
Golden Eagle					r	f,c	f	f	f	
American Kestrel		o	o	o		f,c	f	f	f	
Merlin		r		r		f,c	f	f	f	
Virginia Rail		o	o	r			f,c			
Sora	Y	u	c	o			f,n,c			
American Coot		u	o	u			f,c			
Sandhill Crane		o		o				c	f,c	
Killdeer	Y	c	u	u				f,n,c	f,n,c	
Spotted Sandpiper		o	o	o			f,c			
Common Snipe		r	r	r			f,c			
Bonaparte's Gull		u		u			f,c			
Ring-billed Gull		u	u	u			f,c			
Herring Gull		r		r			f,c			
Rock Dove	Y	c	c	o	o			f	f,c	
Mourning Dove	Y	c	c	c		f,n,c		f,c	f,c	
Black-billed Cuckoo		u	o	o		f,c				
Great-horned Owl		u	u	u	o	f,c	f	f	f	
Barred Owl		o	o	o	o	f,c	f	f	f	

Species (Bold indicates species that are abundant or common on the refuge for at least part of the year)	Nesting? Y=Yes	Status on Refuge (See top of table for codes)				Potential Benefit f=food, n=nesting, c=cover				Status in Region and State (See top for codes)
		Sp	S	Fall	W	Forest	Wet.	Grass.	Crop	
Snowy Owl		r			r	f,c	f	f	f	
Common Nighthawk		o	o	o		f,c	f	f	f	
Whip-poor-will		r	r	r		f,c	f	f	f	
Chimney Swift		r	r	r		f,c	f	f	f	
Ruby-throated Hummingbird	Y	u	c	c		f,n,c		f,c	f,c	
Belted Kingfisher		u	u	u		c	f,c			
Yellow-bellied Sapsucker	Y	o	u	u		f,n,c				
Downy Woodpecker	Y	c	u	u	c	f,n,c				
Hairy Woodpecker	Y	u	u	u	u	f,n,c				
Pileated Woodpecker	Y	u	o	o	u	f,n,c				
Eastern Wood-Pewee		u	c	c		f,c	f	f	f	
Least Flycatcher	Y	u	c	c		f,n,c	f	f	f	
Eastern Phoebe	Y	c	c	c		f,n,c	f	f	f,n,c	
Great Crested Flycatcher	Y	u	c	u		f,n,c	f	f	f,n,c	
Western Kingbird		r				f,c	f	f	f,c	
Eastern Kingbird		u	u	u		f,c	f	f	f,c	
Horned Lark		u	u	u				f,c	f,c	
Purple Martin		r		r		f	f	f	f,c	
Tree Swallow	Y	c	a	a		f,n,c	f	f	f,n,c	
Northern Rough-winged Swallow		o	o	o		f,c	f	f	f,c	
Bank Swallow	Y	u	o	u		f,n,c	f	f	f,n,c	
Cliff Swallow	Y	u	u	u		f,n,c	f	f	f,n,c	
Barn Swallow	Y	c	a	c		f,n,c	f	f	f,n,c	
Blue Jay	Y	c	c	c	c	f,n,c	f	f	f,n,c	
Black-billed Magpie		o	o	o	r	f,c	f	f	f,c	
American Crow	Y	c	c	c	o	f,n,c	f	f	f,n,c	
Common Raven		r			r	f,c	f	f	f,c	
Black-capped Chickadee	Y	o	c	c	a	f,n,c		f	f,n,c	
Red-breasted Nuthatch		o	r	o	o	f,c				
White-breasted Nuthatch	Y	c	c	c	c	f,n,c				

Species (**Bold** indicates species that are abundant or common on the refuge for at least part of the year)	Nesting? Y=Yes	Status on Refuge (See top of table for codes)				Potential Benefit f=food, n=nesting, c=cover				Status in Region and State (See top for codes)
		Sp	S	Fall	W	Forest	Wet.	Grass.	Crop	
Brown Creeper		o	r	o	o	f,c				
House Wren	Y	u	c	u		f,n,c			f,n,c	
Marsh Wren	Y	u	c	u			f,n,c	f,c	f,c	
Golden-crowned Kinglet		r		r		f,c			f,c	
Ruby-crowned Kinglet		o		o		f,c			f,c	
Eastern Bluebird	Y	u	c	u		f,n,c		f,c	f,n,c	
Swainson's Thrush		o		o		f,c			f	
Hermit Thrush		o		o		f,c			f	
American Robin	Y	c	c	c		f,n,c		f,c	f,n,c	
Gray Catbird	Y	u	c	u		f,n,c		f,c	f,n,c	
Brown Thrasher	Y	u	u	u		f,n,c		f,c	f,n,c	
Bohemian Waxwing		r		r		f,c		f	f,c	
Cedar Waxwing	Y	u	u	u	o	f,n,c		f	f,n,c	
Ring-necked Pheasant		r	r	r	r		f,c	f,c	f,c	
Ruffed Grouse	Y	o	u	u	u	f,n,c				
Northern Shrike		r			o	f,c	f	f	f,c	
European Starling		r	r	r	r	f,c		f	f,c	
Solitary Vireo		o	r	o		f,c			f,c	
Yellow-throated Vireo	Y	u	o	u		f,n,c			f,n,c	
Warbling Vireo		u	o	u		f,c			f,c	
Philadelphia Vireo		o	r	o		f,c			f,c	
Red-eyed Vireo	Y	u	c	u		f,n,c			f,n,c	
Tennessee Warbler		o	r	o		f,c			f,c	
Orange-crowned Warbler		o		o		f,c			f,c	
Nashville Warbler		o	r	o		f,c			f,c	
Northern Parula		o		o		f,c			f,c	
Yellow Warbler	Y	c	c	c		f,n,c			f,n,c	
Magnolia Warbler		o		o		f,c			f,c	
Cape May Warbler		o		o		f,c			f,c	
Yellow-rumped Warbler		u		u		f,c			f,c	

Species (Bold indicates species that are abundant or common on the refuge for at least part of the year)	Nesting? Y=Yes	Status on Refuge (See top of table for codes)				Potential Benefit f=food, n=nesting, c=cover				Status in Region and State (See top for codes)
		Sp	S	Fall	W	Forest	Wet.	Grass.	Crop	
Black-throated Green Warbler		o		o		f,c			f,c	
Blackburnian warbler		o		o		f,c			f,c	
Pine Warbler		o		o		f,c			f,c	
Palm Warbler		o		o		f,c			f,c	
Bay-breasted Warbler		o		o		f,c			f,c	
Blackpoll Warbler		o		o		f,c			f,c	
Black-and-white Warbler		o	r	o		f,c			f,c	
American Redstart		o	r	o		f,c			f,c	
Ovenbird	Y	c	c	c		f,n,c			f,n,c	
Connecticut Warbler		r		r		f,c			f,c	
Mourning Warbler		r		r		f,c				
Common Yellowthroat	Y	u	c	u		f,n,c	f,n,c	f,n,c	f,n,c	
Wilson's Warbler		o		o		f,c	f,c		f,c	
Canada Warbler		o		o		f,c			f,c	
Scarlet Tanager	Y	u	o	o		f,n,c			f,n,c	
Rose-breasted Grosbeak	Y	u	o	o		f,n,c			f,n,c	
Rufous-sided Towhee		o		o		f,c			f,c	
Pine Grosbeak		r			r				f,c	
Evening Grosbeak		r			r				f,c	
Blue Grosbeak				r					f,c	
Indigo Bunting		u	o	o		f,c			f,c	
Snow Bunting		r			r				f,c	
American Tree Sparrow		r		r	r	f,c	f,c	f,c	f,c	
House Sparrow	Y	c	c	c	c	f,n,c	f,n,c	f,c	f,n,c	
Chipping sparrow	Y	c	a	c				f,c	f,n,c	
Clay-colored Sparrow	Y	c	a	c		f,n,c		f,c	f,n,c	
Vesper Sparrow	Y	c	c	u		f,n,c		f,c	f,n,c	
Savannah Sparrow	Y	c	c	u				f,c	f,n,c	
LeConte's Sparrow		o	r	o		f,c	f,c			
Sharp-tailed Sparrow		r	r	r		f,c	f,c			

Species (**Bold** indicates species that are abundant or common on the refuge for at least part of the year)	Nesting? Y=Yes	Status on Refuge (See top of table for codes)				Potential Benefit f=food, n=nesting, c=cover				Status in Region and State (See top for codes)
		Sp	S	Fall	W	Forest	Wet.	Grass.	Crop	
Fox Sparrow		o		o		f,c				
Song Sparrow	Y	c	c	c		f,n,c	f,c	f,c	f,n,c	
Lincoln's Sparrow		r		r		f,c	f,c	f,c	f,c	
Swamp Sparrow		u	o	u			f,c	f,c	f,c	
White-throated Sparrow		u	r	u		f,c			f,c	
White-crowned Sparrow		o		o		f,c	f,c	f,c	f,c	
Harris' Sparrow		o		o		f,c	f,c	f,c	f,c	
Dark-eyed Junco		o		o	r	f,c		f,c	f,c	
Western Meadowlark		u	o	u				f,c	f,c	
Red-winged Blackbird	Y	a	a	a	r		f,n,c		f,n,c	
Yellow-headed Blackbird		o		o			f,c			
Rusty Blackbird		r		r	r	f,c			f,c	
Brewer's Blackbird		r		r	r				f,c	
Common Grackle		c	u	c					f,c	
Brown-headed Cowbird		c	u	c					f,c	
Orchard Oriole		r		r		f,c			f,c	
Northern Oriole	Y	u	u	u		f,n,c			f,c	
Purple Finch		u	u	u	u				f,c	
House Finch		o	o	o	o				f,c	
Red Crossbill		r			r				f,c	
White-winged Crossbill		r			r				f,c	
Common Redpoll		r			r	f,c			f,c	
Hoary Redpoll		r			r	f,c			f,c	
Pine Siskin		o	o	o	o				f,c	
American Goldfinch	Y	c	c	c	o	f,n,c			f,n,c	

Appendix G: Compliance Requirements

Appendix G: Compliance Requirements

Rivers and Harbor Act (1899) (33 U.S.C. 403): Section 10 of this Act requires the authorization by the U.S. Army Corps of Engineers prior to any work in, on, over, or under a navigable water of the United States.

Antiquities Act (1906): Authorizes the scientific investigation of antiquities on Federal land and provides penalties for unauthorized removal of objects taken or collected without a permit.

Migratory Bird Treaty Act (1918): Designates the protection of migratory birds as a Federal responsibility. This Act enables the setting of seasons, and other regulations including the closing of areas, Federal or non-Federal, to the hunting of migratory birds.

Migratory Bird Conservation Act (1929): Establishes procedures for acquisition by purchase, rental, or gift of areas approved by the Migratory Bird Conservation Commission.

Fish and Wildlife Coordination Act (1934), as amended: Requires that the Fish and Wildlife Service and State fish and wildlife agencies be consulted whenever water is to be impounded, diverted or modified under a Federal permit or license. The Service and State agency recommend measures to prevent the loss of biological resources, or to mitigate or compensate for the damage. The project proponent must take biological resource values into account and adopt justifiable protection measures to obtain maximum overall project benefits. A 1958 amendment added provisions to recognize the vital contribution of wildlife resources to the Nation and to require equal consideration and coordination of wildlife conservation with other water resources development programs. It also authorized the Secretary of Interior to provide public fishing areas and accept donations of lands and funds.

Migratory Bird Hunting and Conservation Stamp Act (1934): Authorized the opening of part of a refuge to waterfowl hunting.

Historic Sites, Buildings and Antiquities Act (1935), as amended: Declares it a national policy to preserve historic sites and objects of national significance, including those located on refuges. Provides procedures for designation, acquisition, administration, and protection of such sites.

Refuge Revenue Sharing Act (1935), as amended: Requires revenue sharing provisions to all fee-title ownerships that are administered solely or primarily by the Secretary through the Service.

Bald and Golden Eagle Protection Act, 1940

Transfer of Certain Real Property for Wildlife Conservation Purposes Act (1948): Provides that upon a determination by the Administrator of the General Services Administration, real property no longer needed by a Federal agency can be transferred without reimbursement to the Secretary of Interior if the land has particular value for migratory birds, or to a State agency for other wildlife conservation purposes.

Federal Records Act (1950): Directs the preservation of evidence of the government's organization, functions, policies, decisions, operations, and activities, as well as basic historical and other information.

Fish and Wildlife Act (1956): Established a comprehensive national fish and wildlife policy and broadened the authority for acquisition and development of refuges.

Refuge Recreation Act (1962): Allows the use of refuges for recreation when such uses are compatible with the refuge's primary purposes and when sufficient funds are available to manage the uses.

Wilderness Act (1964), as amended: Directed the Secretary of Interior, within 10 years, to review every roadless area of 5,000 or more acres and every roadless island (regardless of size) within National Wildlife Refuge and National Park Systems and to recommend to the President the suitability of each such area or island for inclusion in the National Wilderness Preservation System, with final decisions made by Congress. The Secretary of Agriculture was directed to study and recommend suitable areas in the National Forest System.

Land and Water Conservation Fund Act (1965): Uses the receipts from the sale of surplus Federal land, outer continental shelf oil and gas sales, and other sources for land acquisition under several authorities.

National Wildlife Refuge System Administration Act (1966), as amended by the National Wildlife Refuge System Improvement Act (1997)16 U.S.C. 668dd668ee. (Refuge Administration Act): Defines the National Wildlife Refuge System and authorizes the Secretary to permit any use of a refuge provided such use is compatible with the major purposes for which the refuge was established. The Refuge Improvement Act clearly defines a unifying mission for the Refuge System; establishes the legitimacy and appropriateness of the six priority public uses (hunting, fishing, wildlife observation and photography, or environmental education and interpretation); establishes a formal process for determining compatibility; established the responsibilities of the Secretary of Interior for managing and protecting the System; and requires a Comprehensive Conservation Plan for each refuge by the year 2012. This Act amended portions of the Refuge Recreation Act and National Wildlife Refuge System Administration Act of 1966.

National Historic Preservation Act (1966), as amended: Establishes as policy that the Federal Government is to provide leadership in the preservation of the nation's prehistoric and historic resources.

Architectural Barriers Act (1968): Requires federally owned, leased, or funded buildings and facilities to be accessible to persons with disabilities.

National Environmental Policy Act (1969): Requires the disclosure of the environmental impacts of any major Federal action significantly affecting the quality of the human environment.

Uniform Relocation and Assistance and Real Property Acquisition Policies Act (1970), as amended: Provides for uniform and equitable treatment of persons who sell their homes, businesses, or farms to the Service. The Act requires that any purchase offer be no less than the fair market value of the property.

Clean Air Act, 1970

Endangered Species Act (1973): Requires all Federal agencies to carry out programs for the conservation of endangered and threatened species.

Rehabilitation Act (1973): Requires programmatic accessibility in addition to physical accessibility for all facilities and programs funded by the Federal government to ensure that anybody can participate in any program.

Archaeological and Historic Preservation Act (1974): Directs the preservation of historic and archaeological data in Federal construction projects.

Fishery (Magnuson) Conservation and Management Act, 1976

Clean Water Act (1977): Requires consultation with the Corps of Engineers (404 permits) for major wetland modifications.

Surface Mining Control and Reclamation Act (1977) as amended (Public Law 95-87) (SMCRA): Regulates surface mining activities and reclamation of coal-mined lands. Further regulates the coal industry by designating certain areas as unsuitable for coal mining operations.

Executive Order 11988 (1977): Each Federal agency shall provide leadership and take action to reduce the risk of flood loss and minimize the impact of floods on human safety, and preserve the natural and beneficial values served by the floodplains.

Executive Order 11990: Executive Order 11990 directs Federal agencies to (1) minimize destruction, loss, or degradation of wetlands and (2) preserve and enhance the natural and beneficial values of wetlands when a practical alternative exists.

Executive Order 12372 (Intergovernmental Review of Federal Programs): Directs the Service to send copies of the Environmental Assessment to State Planning Agencies for review.

Executive Order 11644, Use of Off-Road Vehicles on Public Land

Executive Order 12962, Recreational Fisheries

Executive Order 13084, Consultation/Coordination with Tribal Governments

Executive Order 11987, Exotic Organisms

American Indian Religious Freedom Act (1978): Directs agencies to consult with native traditional religious leaders to determine appropriate policy changes necessary to protect and preserve Native American religious cultural rights and practices.

Fish and Wildlife Improvement Act (1978): Improves the administration of fish and wildlife programs and amends several earlier laws including the Refuge Recreation Act, the National Wildlife Refuge System Administration Act, and the Fish and Wildlife Act of 1956. It authorizes the Secretary to accept gifts and bequests of real and personal property on behalf of the United States. It also authorizes the use of volunteers on Service projects and appropriations to carry out a volunteer program.

Archaeological Resources Protection Act (1979), as amended: Protects materials of archaeological interest from unauthorized removal or destruction and requires Federal managers to develop plans and schedules to locate archaeological resources.

Federal Farmland Protection Policy Act (1981), as amended: Minimizes the extent to which Federal programs contribute to the unnecessary and irreversible conversion of farmland to nonagricultural uses.

Emergency Wetlands Resources Act (1986): Promotes the conservation of migratory waterfowl and offsets or prevents the serious loss of wetlands by the acquisition of wetlands and other essential habitats.

Federal Noxious Weed Act (1990): Requires the use of integrated management systems to control or contain undesirable plant species, and an interdisciplinary approach with the cooperation of other Federal and State agencies.

Native American Graves Protection and Repatriation Act (1990): Requires Federal agencies and museums to inventory, determine ownership of, and repatriate cultural items under their control or possession.

Americans With Disabilities Act (1992): Prohibits discrimination in public accommodations and services.

Executive Order 12898 (1994): Establishes environmental justice as a Federal government priority and directs all Federal agencies to make environmental justice part of their mission. Environmental justice calls for fair distribution of environmental hazards.

Executive Order 12996 Management and General Public Use of the National Wildlife Refuge System (1996): Defines the mission, purpose, and priority public uses of the National Wildlife Refuge System. It also presents four principles to guide management of the System.

Executive Order 13007 Indian Sacred Sites (1996): Directs Federal land management agencies to accommodate access to and ceremonial use of Indian sacred sites by Indian religious practitioners, avoid adversely affecting the physical integrity of such sacred sites, and where appropriate, maintain the confidentiality of sacred sites.

National Wildlife Refuge System Improvement Act (1997): Considered the "Organic Act of the National Wildlife Refuge System. Defines the mission of the System, designates priority wildlife-dependent public uses, and calls for comprehensive refuge planning.

National Wildlife Refuge System Volunteer and Community Partnership Enhancement Act (1998): Amends the Fish and Wildlife Act of 1956 to promote volunteer programs and community partnerships for the benefit of national wildlife refuges, and for other purposes.

National Trails System Act: Assigns responsibility to the Secretary of Interior and thus the Service to protect the historic and recreational values of congressionally designated National Historic Trail sites.

Appendix H : Compatibility Determinations

Compatibility Determination

Use: Deer Hunting

Refuge Name: Rydell National Wildlife Refuge

Establishing and Acquisition Authority(ies): The Refuge was established in January 1992 under the Fish and Wildlife Act of 1956, as amended; and Recreational Use of Conservation Areas Act of 1962, as amended.

Refuge Purpose(s): Rydell National Wildlife Refuge was established "... for the development, advancement, management, conservation and protection of fish and wildlife resources... 16 U. S. C. 742f (a) (4) "... for the benefit of the United States Fish and Wildlife Service, in performing its activities and services. Such acceptance may be subject to the terms of any restrictive or affirmative covenant, or condition of servitude ..." 16 U. S. C. 742f(b) (1) (Fish and Wildlife Act of 1956, 16 U. S. C. 742(a) -754, as amended).

National Wildlife Refuge System Mission: The National Wildlife Refuge System mission is to administer a national network of lands and waters for the conservation, management and, where appropriate, restoration of the fish, wildlife and plant resources and their habitats within the United States for the benefit of present and future generations of Americans.

Description of Use:

What is the use? White-tailed deer hunting with special hunts for disabled persons, for first-time hunters less than 16 ("youth hunts") and hunts during the regularly established hunting seasons as necessary, through a drawing. Numbers of hunters allowed access to the Refuge will depend on the estimated desired harvest of deer to maintain the herd within the carrying capacity of the Refuge. Additional special management hunts may be conducted through special drawings and permits.

Where is the use conducted? Deer hunting may occur throughout the Refuge, with vehicle traffic restricted to established roads and trails.

When is the use conducted? The use may occur during the state season for the zone that includes the Refuge or, with state permission, prior to the regular firearm season for persons with disabilities.

How is the use conducted? Hunters are selected from eligible applicants through a drawing. Currently, a special hunt is held for persons with disabilities working with Options: Resource Center for Independent Living in East Grand Forks, Minnesota. When possible, special hunts for young, first-time hunters will also be held during the regular state wide, open deer season. Youth hunts include an onsite training program. If the harvest through the above hunts is determined to be insufficient, we will conduct special management hunts as necessary to maintain the deer herd within the limits of the available habitat.

Availability of Resources: Based on a review of the Refuge budget allocated for this activity, there is sufficient funding available to ensure compatibility and to administer and manage the use at its anticipated level. A failure to conduct regular deer hunts, when necessary, will result in damage the woodland resources of the Refuge, and will make it impossible to restore the forested areas planned.

Anticipated Impacts of the Use: Disturbance to wildlife would temporarily increase during the hunting season. Auto traffic would be restricted to established roads and trails so disturbance to vegetation would be minimal. Some temporary dispersal of animals off of the Refuge may occur. These animals could be harvested by hunters hunting on Waterfowl Production Areas or private lands around the Refuge boundary.

The hunts help control the size of the deer herd, thereby reducing the stresses of disease and parasites and the damaging effects of over population on the Refuge habitat.

Public Review and Comment: This compatibility determination was part of the Draft Rydell National Wildlife Refuge Comprehensive Conservation Plan and Environmental Assessment, which was announced in the Federal Register and available for public comment for 30 days.

Determination:

      ___Use is Not Compatible
      _X_ Use is Compatible with the Following Stipulations

Stipulations Necessary to Ensure Compatibility: To ensure compatibility with National Wildlife Refuge System and Rydell National Wildlife Refuge goals and objectives, hunting will only occur under the following stipulations:

1. Hunting will occur under a system of limited permits to ensure that a) the harvest does not have an adverse effect on the Refuge's deer population, b) disturbance of non target species is minimized, and c) activities can be conducted in a safe manner for participants and area residents.

2. Annually, we will a) review all hunting activities and operations to ensure compliance with all applicable laws, regulations, and policies and b) apply to the Minnesota Department of Natural Resources for special hunt permits.

Justification: Allowing deer hunting on Rydell National Wildlife Refuge, within the stipulations above, will have a positive effect on the wildlife life resources of the Refuge. Deer populations need to be kept within the carrying capacity of the existing habitat. Failure to maintain the deer herd within the population capacity of the Refuge will result in serious degradation of the woodland and upland habitats, thereby impacting the other wildlife residents of the Refuge.

Signature:

Refuge Manager: _s/Richard Julian_____ Date: _September 21, 2001_
                Refuge Manager

Concurrence: _ s/Nita M. Fuller_____Date: _September 28, 2001_
                Regional Chief, National Wildlife Refuge System

Mandatory 10- or 15-year Re-evaluation Date: 2016

Compatibility Determination

Use: Waterfowl Hunting

Refuge Name: Rydell National Wildlife Refuge

Establishing and Acquisition Authority(ies): Rydell National Wildlife Refuge was established in January 1992 under the authority of the Fish and Wildlife Act of 1956, as amended; and Recreational Use of Conservation Areas Act of 1962, as amended.

Refuge Purpose(s): Rydell National Wildlife Refuge was established "... for the development, advancement, management, conservation and protection of fish and wildlife resources... 16 U. S. C. 742f (a) (4)   "... for the benefit of the United States Fish and Wildlife Service, in performing its activities and services. Such acceptance may be subject to the terms of any restrictive or affirmative covenant, or condition of servitude ..." 16 U. S. C. 742f(b) (1) (Fish and Wildlife Act of 1956, 16 U. S. C. 742(a) -754, as amended).

National Wildlife Refuge System Mission: The National Wildlife Refuge System mission is to administer a national network of lands and waters for the conservation, management and, where appropriate, restoration of the fish, wildlife and plant resources and their habitats within the United States for the benefit of present and future generations of Americans.

Description of Use:

What is the use? Waterfowl hunting.

Where is the use conducted? Hunting will occur in designated areas of the Refuge.

When is the use conducted? All hunting will follow applicable state seasons, except where the Refuge administers further restrictions to ensure compatibility with the Refuge's primary mission.

How is the use conducted? A step-down hunting plan will describe the details of the hunting program. Each year the plan will be reviewed and any changes submitted for approval. All hunting will be planned and operated with the Refuge's primary objectives, habitat management requirements and goals as the guiding principles. All hunting activities will follow applicable state laws, except where the Refuge administers further restrictions to ensure compatibility with the Refuge's primary mission. Hunting activities will only occur in designated areas. Hunting activities are intended to meet the National Wildlife Refuge System Improvement Act and some of the Refuge objectives and management goals without adversely affecting the primary objectives and mission of the refuge. Completing this activity under a hunting plan and special permit allows the Refuge to accomplish its management goals and provide needed safety levels for citizens of the area without adversely affecting Refuge habitats and wildlife populations.

Availability of Resources: Funds are available for managing this activity. Approximately $2,600 of staff time will be required to administer and manage this activity. It is estimated an additional $500 is required for overhead expenses associated with this activity for a total estimated cost of $3,100 to administer the program. Based on a review of the Refuge budget there are not adequate resources to administer and manage this use at the present time.

Anticipated Impacts of the Use: As envisioned this activity will have no assessable environmental impact to the Refuge, its habitats or wildlife species. With restrictions limiting access to specific locations, disturbance is minimized. Waterfowl hunting would only occur at designated locations within the Refuge with 70 percent of the core acreage left undisturbed. Disturbance to wildlife is limited to occasional flushing of non target species and the harvest of individual members of the species open to the hunting season only. Restrictions to the hunting program assure that these activities have no adverse impacts on other wildlife species and little adverse impact to other public use programs. The activities follow all applicable laws, regulations and policies; including Migratory Bird Conservation Act, 50 CFR, National Wildlife Refuge System Manual, National Wildlife Refuge System goals and objectives, and Rydell NWR goals and objectives. These activities are compliant with the purpose of the Refuge and the National Wildlife Refuge System Mission. Operating this activity does not alter the Refuge's ability to meet habitat goals, provides for the safety of the areas' citizens, and supports several of the primary objectives of the Refuge.

Hunting is a priority public use listed in the National Wildlife Refuge System Improvement Act. By facilitating hunting on the Refuge, we will increase knowledge and appreciation of wildlife among program participants, which will lead to increased public stewardship of wildlife and their habitats at the Refuge and in general. Increased public stewardship will support and complement the Service's actions in achieving the Refuge's purposes and the mission of the National Wildlife Refuge System.

Public Review and Comment: This compatibility determination was part of the Draft Rydell National Wildlife Refuge Comprehensive Conservation Plan and Environmental Assessment, which was announced in the Federal Register and available for public comment for 30 days.

Determination:
>   ____Use is Not Compatible
>   X Use is Compatible with the Following Stipulations

Stipulations Necessary to Ensure Compatibility: To ensure compatibility with National Wildlife Refuge System and Rydell NWR goals and objectives the activity can only occur under the following stipulations:

1. Ensure waterfowl hunting is limited to a maximum of 30 percent of all Refuge acreage and located in the periphery areas along the boundary of the Refuge.

2. Annually review all hunting activities and operations to ensure compliance with all applicable laws, regulations and policies.

Justification: Allowing waterfowl hunting on Rydell National Wildlife Refuge, within the stipulations above, will have minimal impact on the wildlife life resources of the Refuge. Harvesting a small portion of the waterfowl utilizing the Refuge lands will not diminish the primary Refuge purposes of waterfowl production, or the conservation of other migratory birds and wildlife on the refuge.

Signature:

Refuge Manager: s/Richard Julian _____ Date: September 21, 2001
                      Refuge Manager

Concurrence: s/Nita M. Fuller _____ Date: September 28, 2001
                      Regional Chief, National Wildlife Refuge System

Mandatory 10- or 15-year Re-evaluation Date: 2016

Compatibility Determination

Use: Fishing

Refuge Name: Rydell National Wildlife Refuge

Establishing and Acquisition Authority(ies): Rydell National Wildlife Refuge was established in January 1992 under the authority of the Fish and Wildlife Act of 1956, as amended; and Recreational Use of Conservation Areas Act of 1962, as amended.

Refuge Purpose(s): Rydell National Wildlife Refuge was established "... for the development, advancement, management, conservation and protection of fish and wildlife resources... 16 U. S. C. 742f (a) (4) "... for the benefit of theUnited States Fish and Wildlife Service, in performing its activities and services. Such acceptance may be subject to the terms of any restrictive or affirmative covenant, or condition of servitude ..." 16 U. S. C. 742f(b) (1) (Fish and Wildlife Act of 1956, 16 U. S. C. 742(a) -754, as amended).

National Wildlife Refuge System Mission: The National Wildlife Refuge System mission is to administer a national network of lands and waters for the conservation, management and, where appropriate, restoration of the fish, wildlife and plant resources and their habitats within the United States for the benefit of present and future generations of Americans.

Description of Use:

What is the use? Fishing in designated areas of the Refuge.

Where is the use conducted? Fishing activities are restricted to access from the established accessible fishing pier and in areas designated by the Refuge.

When is the use conducted? The use occurs in May, June and July within state regulations.

How is the use conducted? All fishing activities follow applicable state laws, except where the Refuge administers further restrictions to ensure compatibility with the Refuge's primary mission.

Availability of Resources: Funds are available for managing this activity. Approximately $700 of staff time is required to administer and manage this activity. Overhead expenses associated with this activity are estimated to be $500 for a total estimated cost of $1,200 to administer the program. Based on a review of the Refuge budget allocated for this use management activity, there is currently enough funding to ensure compatibility and to administer and manage the use. This activity will only be permitted if funding sources continue to be available to cover the overhead cost for the program.

Anticipated Impacts of the Use: Allowing this activity will not likely result in assessable environmental impact to the Refuge, its habitats or wildlife species. Concerns primarily center around the possibility of impacting non target species through excessive disturbance. With restrictions limiting access to one specific portion of the Refuge and on use of motor boats, disturbance is minimized. Disturbance to wildlife is limited to occasional flushing of non target species and the harvest of individual members of the species open to the recreational fishing. Harvests during fishing activities are covered by state regulations. Restrictions to the fishing program will assure that this activity has no adverse impacts on other wildlife species and little adverse impact to other public use programs. The activities follow all applicable laws, regulations and policies; including Migratory Bird Conservation Act, 50 CFR, National Wildlife Refuge System Manual, National Wildlife Refuge System goals and objectives, and Rydell NWR goals and objectives. These activities are consistent with the purpose of the Refuge and the National Wildlife Refuge System Mission.

Fishing is a priority public use listed in the National Wildlife Refuge System Improvement Act. By facilitating fishing on the Refuge, we will increase knowledge and appreciation of fish and wildlife among program participants, which will lead to increased public stewardship of wildlife and their habitats at the Refuge and in general. Increased public stewardship will support and complement the Service's actions in achieving the Refuge's purposes and the mission of the National Wildlife Refuge System.

Public Review and Comment: This compatibility determination was part of the Draft Rydell National Wildlife Refuge Comprehensive Conservation Plan and Environmental Assessment, which was announced in the Federal Register and available for public comment for 30 days.

Determination:

    ___Use is Not Compatible
     X Use is Compatible with the Following Stipulations

Stipulations Necessary to Ensure Compatibility: To ensure compatibility with National Wildlife Refuge System and Rydell NWR goals and objectives the activity can only occur under the following stipulations:

1. All fishing activities can only occur in designated locations using specific routes for access thus ensuring disturbance to wildlife species is minimized and activities are operated with minimal impacts to wildlife and habitats.

2. All fishing activities are operated under state laws unless the Refuge places further restrictions on the activities to ensure compliance with all applicable laws, regulations and policies.

Justification: Allowing limited fishing on Rydell National Wildlife Refuge, within the stipulations above, will have minimal impact on the wildlife life resources of the Refuge. Vegetative cover in the immediate vicinity of the fishing pier is quite rank. Wood duck and mallard broods could frequent the area for feeding purposes during June and July. Adequate cover exists in the area where temporarily displaced birds will find adequate food and cover. Fish populations subject to harvest will be migrating out of Maple Lake, a 4-mile-long body of water immediately west of the Refuge. Fishing will only be effective during the early summer before water levels drop to summer lows and aquatic vegetation growth eliminates fishing opportunities.

Signature:

Refuge Manager: s/Richard Julian_____Date: September 21, 2001
                    Refuge Manager

Concurrence: s/Nita M. Fuller_____Date: September 28, 2001
                    Regional Chief, National Wildlife Refuge System

Mandatory 10- or 15-year Re-evaluation Date: 2016

Compatibility Determination

Use: Wildlife Observation and Photography

Refuge Name: Rydell National Wildlife Refuge

Establishing and Acquisition Authority(ies): Rydell National Wildlife Refuge was established in January 1992 under the authority of the Fish and Wildlife Act of 1956, as amended; and Recreational Use of Conservation Areas Act of 1962, as amended.

Refuge Purpose(s): Rydell National Wildlife Refuge was established "... for the development, advancement, management, conservation and protection of fish wildlife resources... 16 U. S. C. 742f (a) (4) "... for the benefit of the States Fish and Wildlife Service, in performing its activities and services. Such acceptance may be subject to the terms of any restrictive or affirmative covenant, or condition of servitude ..." 16 U. S. C. 742f(b) (1) (Fish and Wildlife Act of 1956, 16 U. S. C. 742(a) -754, as amended).

National Wildlife Refuge System Mission: The National Wildlife Refuge System mission is to administer a national network of lands and waters for the conservation, management and, where appropriate, restoration of the fish, wildlife and plant resources and their habitats within the United States for the benefit of present and future generations of Americans.

Description of Use:

What is the use? Wildlife observation and photography

Where is the use conducted? Currently, wildlife observation and photography occur along and near the existing 7 miles of accessible trails in the northeast portion of the Refuge and at observation overlooks and boardwalks. Occasionally auto tours are conducted on portions of the Refuge road system. The CCP calls for developing an auto access tour route through the northern portion of the Refuge along existing refuge roads and the development of one half mile of rerouted road.

When is the use conducted? The use occurs year-round and is dependent on access.

How is the use conducted? Access for wildlife observation and photography is gained through walking, bicycling, snowshoeing and cross-country skiing on designated trails, by automobile on Refuge roads, and by non-motorized canoe in designated areas outside the waterfowl nesting season. As an accommodation to people with disabilities, electric carts will be available for use on designated portions of trails. The new auto tour route would be open during designated hours from late spring through summer, depending on wildlife use and road conditions.

Availability of Resources: Based on a review of the Refuge budget allocated for this activity, there is adequate funding to ensure compatibility and to administer and manage the use at its current level. Approximately $1,000 of staff time and

---

$500 of overhead is required to administer this use. Establishing the auto tour route has been submitted for funding within the Refuge Operating Needs System.

Anticipated Impacts of the Use: Anticipated impacts from visitors engaged in wildlife observation and photography is minor damage to vegetation, littering, increased maintenance activity, and minor disturbances to wildlife. Because visitors are limited to designated trail access and time limitations may be imposed, wildlife observation and photography have only minor impacts on wildlife and does not detract from the primary purposes of the Refuge. All other potential impacts are considered minor.

Wildlife observation and photography are priority public uses listed in the National Wildlife Refuge System Improvement Act. By facilitating these uses on the Refuge, we will increase visitors' knowledge and appreciation of fish and wildlife, which will lead to increased public stewardship of wildlife and their habitats at the Refuge and in general. Increased public stewardship will support and complement the Service's actions in achieving the Refuge's purposes and the mission of the National Wildlife Refuge System.

Public Review and Comment: This compatibility determination is part of the Draft Rydell National Wildlife Refuge Comprehensive Conservation Plan and Environmental Assessment, which will be announced in the Federal Register and available for public comment for 30 days.

Determination:

　　　___Use is Not Compatible
　　　_X_ Use is Compatible with the Following Stipulations

Stipulations Necessary to Ensure Compatibility: Public access for wildlife observation and photography will be limited to designated areas and with time restrictions to assure minimal disturbance to wildlife and minimal conflict between user groups. Wildlife observation and photography activities will be reviewed annually to ensure this compatibility determination still applies.

Justification: No permanent loss of wildlife habitats will occur as a result of the utilization of portions of the Refuge for wildlife observation and photography programs. Wildlife displaced by such activities will move into the heavy cover along the trail system, away from the disturbance. Space and time limitations placed on wildlife observation/photography opportunities within the Refuge assure that this activity has only minor impacts on wildlife and is consistent with the primary purposes of the Refuge.

Signatures:

Refuge Manager: s/Richard Julian_____Date: September 21, 2001
　　　　　　　Refuge Manager

Concurrence: s/Nita M. Fuller_____Date: September 28, 2001
　　　　　　　Regional Chief, National Wildlife Refuge System

Mandatory 10- or 15-year Re-evaluation Date: 2016

Compatibility Determination

Use: Environmental Education and Interpretation

Refuge Name: Rydell National Wildlife Refuge

Establishing and Acquisition Authority(ies): Rydell National Wildlife Refuge was established in January 1992 under the Fish and Wildlife Act of 1956, as amended; and Recreational Use of Conservation Areas Act of 1962, as amended.

Refuge Purpose(s): Rydell National Wildlife Refuge was established "... for the development, advancement, management, conservation and protection of fish and wildlife resources... 16 U. S. C. 742f (a) (4) "... for the benefit of theUnited States Fish and Wildlife Service, in performing its activities and services. Such acceptance may be subject to the terms of any restrictive or affirmative covenant, or condition of servitude ..." 16 U. S. C. 742f(b) (1) (Fish and Wildlife Act of 1956, 16 U. S. C. 742(a) -754, as amended).

National Wildlife Refuge System Mission: The National Wildlife Refuge System mission is to administer a national network of lands and waters for the conservation, management and, where appropriate, restoration of the fish, wildlife and plant resources and their habitats within the United States for the benefit of present and future generations of Americans.

Description of Use:

What is the use? Environmental education consists of activities conducted by Refuge staff, volunteers, and teachers. Interpretation occurs in a less formal setting with Refuge staff and volunteers or through exhibits, signs, and brochures.

Where is the use conducted? Currently, environmental education and interpretation are conducted within the visitor's center or along the trail system. Facilities at the site will consist of a visitor's center, restroom, benches, Refuge roads, restored fields, 7 miles of accessible trail and boardwalk, bus parking and picnic tables in the northeast portion of the Refuge. These facilities permit school groups to maximize their time at the Refuge in environmental education activities during a limited school day and during summer visits. The remainder of the Refuge serves as a sanctuary for wildlife.

When is the use conducted? The use occurs year-round with peak use in the spring and fall for environmental education with schools and Soil and Water Conservation Districts scheduling many envirothons and other field days.

How is the use conducted? Environmental education activities on the Refuge are led by Refuge staff, volunteers, or teachers, who have been oriented to appropriate use on the Refuge. Students are guided through their activities with adult supervision. Interpretive programs are led by Refuge staff and volunteers. Interpretive materials are developed and placed by Refuge staff.

Availability of Resources: Based on a review of the Refuge budget allocated for this activity, there is some funding available to ensure compatibility and to administer and manage the use at its anticipated level. Approximately $6,000 of staff time and $3,000 of overhead is required to administer this use. Expanding environmental education and interpretation will require the addition of outreach personnel and restroom facilities.

Anticipated Impacts of the Use: Anticipated impacts from environmental education and interpretation are minor damage to vegetation, littering, noise pollution and increased maintenance activity. Minor disturbances to wildlife will occur. Wildlife displaced will move into other portions of the Refuge away from the disturbance. Space and time limitations placed on environmental education and interpretation assure that this activity has only minor impacts on wildlife and is consistent with the primary purposes of the Refuge.

Environmental education is a priority public use listed in the National Wildlife Refuge System Improvement Act. By facilitating environmental education on the Refuge, we will increase knowledge and appreciation of fish and wildlife among program participants, which will lead to increased public stewardship of wildlife and their habitats at the Refuge and in general. Increased public stewardship will support and complement the Service's actions in achieving the Refuge's purposes and the mission of the National Wildlife Refuge System.

Public Review and Comment: This compatibility determination was part of the Draft Rydell National Wildlife Refuge Comprehensive Conservation Plan and Environmental Assessment, which was announced in the Federal Register and available for public comment for 30 days.

Determination:

      ___ Use is Not Compatible

      _X_ Use is Compatible with the Following Stipulations

Stipulations Necessary to Ensure Compatibility: Environmental education will only occur in developed areas designated by the CCP or under the guidance of a Refuge staff member, volunteer, or trained teachers to assure minimal disturbance to wildlife, minimal vegetation damage, and minimal conflict between user groups. Environmental education activities will be reviewed annually to ensure this compatibility determination still applies.

Justification: No permanent loss of wildlife habitat will occur as a result of utilization of portions of the Refuge for environmental education programs. Wildlife displaced will move into other portions of the Refuge away from the disturbance. Space and time limitations placed on environmental education and interpretation assure that this activity has only minor impacts on wildlife and is consistent with the primary purposes of the Refuge. In addition, the long-term educational benefits derived from the on-site programs should benefit the wildlife resources off the Refuge.

Signature:

Refuge Manager: s/Richard Julian   Date: September 21, 2001
          Refuge Manager

Concurrence: s/Nita M. Fuller   Date: September 28, 2001
          Regional Chief, National Wildlife Refuge System

Mandatory 10- or 15-year Re-evaluation Date: 2016

Compatibility Determination

Use: Fish rearing

Refuge Name: Rydell National Wildlife Refuge

Establishing and Acquisition Authority(ies): Rydell National Wildlife Refuge was established in January 1992 under the Fish and Wildlife Act of 1956, as amended; and Recreational Use of Conservation Areas Act of 1962, as amended.

Refuge Purpose(s): Rydell National Wildlife Refuge was established "... for the development, advancement, management, conservation and protection of fish and wildlife resources... 16 U. S. C. 742f (a) (4) "... for the benefit of the United States Fish and Wildlife Service, in performing its activities and services. Such acceptance may be subject to the terms of any restrictive or affirmative covenant, or condition of servitude ..." 16 U. S. C. 742f(b) (1) (Fish and Wildlife Act of 1956, 16 U. S. C. 742(a) -754, as amended).

National Wildlife Refuge System Mission: The National Wildlife Refuge System mission is to administer a national network of lands and waters for the conservation, management and, where appropriate, restoration of the fish, wildlife and plant resources and their habitats within the United States for the benefit of present and future generations of Americans.

Description of Use:

What is the use? Raise walleye fingerlings from fry.

Where is the use conducted? Clifford Lake

When is the use conducted? Fry are placed in the lake in the spring and removed as fingerlings in the fall.

How is the use conducted? The activities associated with fish rearing are conducted by the Service's Division of Fisheries.

Availability of Resources: Based on a review of the Refuge budget allocated for this activity, there is sufficient funding available to ensure compatibility and to administer and manage the use.

Anticipated Impacts of the Use: There will be a limited amount of disturbance caused by access and collection of fingerlings, because the activity is infrequent. Some waterfowl production may be reduced because the walleye fry may reduce the early spring invertebrate population in the lake before they start eating minnows. Reduction of the minnow population may increase available invertebrates for diving ducks during the fall migration.

The program provides approximately between 8,000 and 20,000 walleye fingerlings to Service and Tribal lands each year.

Public Review and Comment:

This compatibility determination was part of the Draft Rydell National Wildlife Refuge Comprehensive Conservation Plan and Environmental Assessment, which was announced in the Federal Register and available for public comment for 30 days.

Determination:

      ___Use is Not Compatible

      _X_Use is Compatible with the Following Stipulations

Stipulations Necessary to Ensure Compatibility: Fish rearing will only occur in Clifford Lake and its effects on waterfowl productivity will be evaluated.

Justification: Allowing fish rearing on Rydell National Wildlife Refuge, within the stipulation above, will have minimal impact on the wildlife life resources of the Refuge. Waterfowl use of Clifford Lake has not appeared to suffer for the current ongoing use of the lake for rearing purposes. A normal complement of breeding waterfowl, equal to that found on wetlands of similar size on the Refuge, are observed on wetlands each year and the lake is the main gathering location for migratory diving ducks and Canada geese each spring and fall. The waterfowl heavily utilize the fresh water shrimp found in this wetland.

Signatures:

Refuge Manager: s/Richard Julian_____Date: September 21, 2001
               Refuge Manager

Concurrence: _s/Nita M. Fuller_____Date: September 28, 2001
               Regional Chief, National Wildlife Refuge System

Mandatory 10- or 15-year Re-evaluation Date: 2011

Compatibility Determination

Use: On Site Research Activities

Refuge Name: Rydell National Wildlife Refuge

Establishing and Acquisition Authority(ies): The Refuge was established in January 1992 under the Fish and Wildlife Act of 1956, as amended; and Recreational Use of Conservation Areas Act of 1962, as amended.

Refuge Purpose(s): Rydell National Wildlife Refuge was established "... for the development, advancement, management, conservation and protection of fish and wildlife resources... 16 U. S. C. 742f (a) (4) "... for the benefit of theUnited States Fish and Wildlife Service, in performing its activities and services. Such acceptance may be subject to the terms of any restrictive or affirmative covenant, or condition of servitude ..." 16 U. S. C. 742f(b) (1) (Fish and Wildlife Act of 1956, 16 U. S. C. 742(a) -754, as amended).

National Wildlife Refuge System Mission: The National Wildlife Refuge System mission is to administer a national network of lands and waters for the conservation, management and, where appropriate, restoration of the fish, wildlife and plant resources and their habitats within the United States for the benefit of present and future generations of Americans.

Description of Use:

Allow local Universities to conduct wildlife and habitat related, or human resources related research activities within the Refuge. The research would be conducted within the woodlands, newly establish prairie restorations, and wetland habitats on the Refuge. Research activities could occur during all time periods of the year.

Written research proposals will be required for review and approval before access will be allowed. If approved, access to Refuge lands and waters will be limited to least invasive means required to accomplish the activities. All land disturbances will be at the minimal level necessary to accomplish goals of the proposed research. Access to study locations off-road will be by foot for land locations and non motorized water craft, if possible.

Availability of Resources: Based on a review of the Refuge budget allocated for this activity, there is sufficient funding available to ensure compatibility and to administer and manage the use at its anticipated level.

Anticipated Impacts of the Use: Disturbance or removal of plants and wildlife would be a temporary impact. Repopulation of the removed individuals would be anticipated to occur over time. Auto traffic would be restricted to established roads and trails so disturbance to vegetation would be minimal. Some temporary dispersal of animals around or off of the Refuge may occur from field activities. Information collected will assist the Refuge manager in fine tuning Refuge management activities to maximize the productivity of the Refuge lands.

Public Review and Comment: This compatibility determination was part of the Draft Rydell National Wildlife Refuge Comprehensive Conservation Plan and

Environmental Assessment, which was announced in the Federal Register and available for public comment for 30 days.

Determination:

     ___Use is Not Compatible

     _X_Use is Compatible with the Following Stipulations

Stipulations Necessary to Ensure Compatibility: To ensure compatibility with National Wildlife Refuge System and Rydell National Wildlife Refuge goals and objectives, on-site research will only occur under the following stipulations:

1. All research proposals will be review for their potential benefits to future Refuge management activities and potential impact(s) to current Refuge purposes. Coordination will be maintained with the Regional Wildlife Biologist on all proposals.

2. Annually, we will all ongoing activities and operations to ensure compliance with all applicable laws, regulations, and policies.

Justification: Allowing wildlife research, within the stipulations above, should result in long-term benefits to the wildlife populations of Rydell National Wildlife Refuge. The collection of detailed information on the habitats and wildlife species within the Refuge is integral to being able to maximize the habitat benefits of the existing landscape for the wildlife species utilizing the Refuge lands.

Signature:

Refuge Manager: <u>s/Richard Julian</u>   Date: <u>September 21, 2001</u>
                      Refuge Manager

Concurrence: <u>s/Nita M. Fuller</u>   Date: <u>September 28, 2001</u>
                      Regional Chief, National Wildlife Refuge System

Mandatory 10- or 15-year Re-evaluation Date: 2011

Compatibility Determination

Use: On-site farming for wildlife observation and no-till demonstration

Refuge Name: Rydell National Wildlife Refuge

Establishing and Acquisition Authority(ies): Rydell National Wildlife Refuge was established in January 1992 under the authority of the Fish and Wildlife Act of 1956, as amended; and Recreational Use of Conservation Areas Act of 1962, as amended.

Refuge Purpose(s): Rydell National Wildlife Refuge was established "... for the development, advancement, management, conservation and protection of fish and wildlife resources... 16 U. S. C. 742f (a) (4) "... for the benefit of theUnited States Fish and Wildlife Service, in performing its activities and services. Such acceptance may be subject to the terms of any restrictive or affirmative covenant, or condition of servitude ..." 16 U. S. C. 742f(b) (1) (Fish and Wildlife Act of 1956, 16 U. S. C. 742(a) -754, as amended).

National Wildlife Refuge System Mission: The National Wildlife Refuge System mission is to administer a national network of lands and waters for the conservation, management and, where appropriate, restoration of the fish, wildlife and plant resources and their habitats within the United States for the benefit of present and future generations of Americans.

Description of Use:

Farming is the term used for cropping activities done by a third party on land that is owned by the Service in fee title. The crop will be harvested annually. This activity on the Refuge will be conducted on a 40-acre parcel of land for the purpose of demonstrating no-till farming approaches to crop productions that have been shown to positively impact waterfowl production by providing additional nesting habitats. As planned, a centrally located crop field will also significantly enhance wildlife observation opportunities for individuals accessing the Refuge trail system.

The cropping will be done under the terms and conditions of a Cooperative Farming Agreement or Special Use Permit issued by the Refuge Manager if a cooperator can be found. The terms of the Agreement or Permit insure that all current Service restrictions are followed. If a cooperator cannot be found, the Refuge is prepared to explore cropping it ourselves.

Availability of Resources: The needed staff time for development and administration of cooperative farming programs is already committed and available. The additional time needed to coordinate issuance and oversight of the needed Special Use Permit or Cooperative Farming Agreement is relatively minor and within existing Refuge resources. It is the Refuge's intention to work with the local USDA office to find an individual who would be willing to utilize his or her no-till equipment to plant on the Refuge lands. Given the small size of the field it may not be possible to find a cooperator. If that occurs, the Service will work with the Friends Association to rent the equipment and plant the crops with the Friends being the partners on the Coop agreement.

The cooperative farming of this small portion of land will not likely generate income for the Service, given the restrictions on using no-till farming equipment. In accordance with Service policy, if income is generated, it will be submitted for deposit in the Refuge Revenue Sharing Account. Generation of income will be a secondary consideration when developing the terms and conditions of a cooperative farming agreement.

To lessen any appearance of favoritism or impropriety in selecting the cooperator, the Refuge manager will document how the cooperator was selected and how the rental rate was derived (see Refuge Manual).

Anticipated Impacts of the Use: Short-term impacts will include disturbance and displacement typical of farming equipment operations during the planting and harvest operations. Continuing cropping activities will result in 40 acres (1.9 percent of the Refuge) not being returned to permanent grassland or woodland habitats for any animal or insect species that would use such areas for nesting, feeding, or resting. Long-term benefits will be in demonstrating the feasibility of cropping with no-till systems in this portion of Minnesota. The use of no-till soybeans has been shown to be an approach to increasing mallard production. The additional benefit to be derived will be more wildlife observation opportunities as wildlife use the harvested field as a feeding area during the fall, winter and spring.

Public Review and Comment: This compatibility determination was made available at Rydell Refuge office and Visitors Center and the local USDA office and posted on the Service web site.

Determination:
       ___Use is Not Compatible
      _X_ Use is Compatible with the Following Stipulations

Stipulations Necessary to Ensure Compatibility: To ensure compatibility with National Wildlife Refuge System and Rydell National Wildlife Refuge goals and objectives, crop production will only occur under the following stipulations:

Annually, we will review all ongoing activities and operations to ensure compliance with all applicable laws, regulations, and policies.

Justification: Cooperative farming will result in annual, short-term disturbances, but there will be long-term benefits to resident and migratory wildlife and increased appreciation of wildlife. By demonstrating no-till techniques, we will encourage farmers in the community to adopt a technique that has a proven beneficial effect on waterfowl production in comparison to conventional techniques. By facilitating wildlife observation, one of the priority public uses, we will encourage increased appreciation of wildlife. Limited cropping activities should result in long-term benefits to the wildlife populations of Rydell National Wildlife Refuge and the surrounding agricultural community and is a prudent activity for a Refuge identified as a demonstration site. The long-term benefits gained though demonstration and increased public appreciation of wildlife exceed the short term losses incurred through the cropping process and the natural habitat foregone on less than 2 percent of the Refuge's acreage.

Signature:

Refuge Manager: s/Richard Julian_____Date: September 21, 2001
                        Refuge Manager

Concurrence: s/Nita M. Fuller_____ Date: September 28, 2001
                        Regional Chief, National Wildlife Refuge System

Mandatory 10- or 15-year Re-evaluation Date: 2011

Appendix I: Environmental Assessment

Finding of No Significant Impact

Environmental Assessment and Comprehensive Conservation Plan for the Rydell National Wildlife Refuge, Minnesota

An Environmental Assessment (EA) has been prepared to identify management strategies to meet the conservation goals of the Rydell National Wildlife Refuge (Rydell Refuge). The EA examined the environmental consequences that each management alternative could have on the quality of the physical, biological, and human environment, as required by the National Environmental Policy Act of 1969 (NEPA). The EA presented and evaluated two alternatives for managing fish, wildlife and plant habitats, as well as visitor services, on the Rydell Refuge for the next 15 years.

Alternative A. No Action (Current Management). The No Action alternative encouraged existing, or status quo, refuge management practices. Changes in land use/cover and visitor services would continue at current rates. The Refuge would maintain its coordination and cooperation with partners. Water quality activities off-Refuge would be very limited.

Alternative B. Implement the Comprehensive Conservation Plan. This alternative emphasized an accelerated schedule for restoration of wetlands, development of a full cadre of volunteers, a proactive role in addressing water quality issues that originate outside the Refuge, and wildlife-dependent recreation that is accessible to people of all abilities. Under this alternative most of the Refuge's cropland would be converted to native grassland and forest.

Under both alternatives obligations for cultural resource management and threatened and endangered species would be met.

The alternative selected for implementation is *Alternative B*. Habitats will be managed for nesting and migrating waterfowl and songbirds. Thus, habitat management will benefit a variety of fish and wildlife plant species identified as Resource Conservation Priority species by the Service. Visitors to the Refuge will also benefit from higher quality, accessible facilities and programs. Water quality in the wetlands and, especially, Maple Lake will improve as algae growth decreases in the lakes. And, the Refuge will experience an ever increasing base of community involvement and support.

For reasons presented above and below, and based on an evaluation of the information contained in the Environmental Assessment, we have determined that the action of adopting Alternative B as the management alternative for the Rydell Refuge CCP is not a major federal action which would significantly affect the quality of the human environment, within the meaning of Section 102 (2)(c) of the National Environmental Policy Act of 1969.

Additional Reasons:

1. Future management actions will have a neutral or positive impact on the local economy.

2. A cultural resource inventory completed prior to this CCP included recommendations for the protection of cultural, archaeological and historical resources.

3. This action will not have an adverse impact on threatened or endangered species.

Supporting References:

Environmental Assessment
Comprehensive Conservation Plan

ACTING _____ ____9/28/01____
Regional Director   Date
   Marvin E. Moriarty

Great Lakes - Big Rivers Region
Bishop Henry Whipple Federal Building
Fort Snelling, MN 55111-4056

Contents

Abstract 117
I. Purpose and Need for the Proposed Action 118
Purpose of Action 118
Need for Action 118
Decisions that Need to be Made 118
Scoping of the Issues 118
Issues and Concerns 118
Authority, Legal Compliance and Compatibility 119
Background 120

II. Description of Alternatives 121
1. Alternatives Eliminated from Consideration 121
2. Alternatives Considered 121
Alternative 1 – No Action 122
Alternative 2 – Implement the CCP (Preferred Alternative) 123

III. Affected Environment 124

IV. Environmental Consequences 126
Effects Common to Both Alternatives 126
Alternative 1 – No Action 127
Alternative 2 – Implement the CCP (Preferred Alternative) 127

V. List of Preparers 130

List of Tables

Table 1: Habitat Conversion 125
Table 2: Comparison of Alternatives (By Year 2012) 126
Table 3: Summary of Consequences Under Alternatives 129

Environmental Assessment
for the
Rydell National Wildlife Refuge
Comprehensive Conservation Plan

December 2000

Abstract

The U.S. Fish and Wildlife Service is proposing to implement the Comprehensive Conservation Plan (CCP) for the Rydell National Wildlife Refuge (Refuge) in Polk County of northwestern Minnesota. The CCP will guide management for the next 15 years. A long-term management direction does not currently exist for Rydell National Wildlife Refuge. Management is now guided by general policies and shorter-term plans. Two alternatives for future Refuge management are described—the status quo and an expanded program of habitat restoration and partnerships. Our preferred alternative is identified as the expanded program. This Environmental Assessment considers the biological, environmental and socioeconomic effects that the two alternatives would have on the most significant issues and concerns identified during the planning process.

Responsible Agency and Official:

William Hartwig, Regional Director
U. S. Fish and Wildlife Service
Henry Whipple Federal Building
1 Federal Drive
Fort Snelling, MN   55111-4056

Contacts for additional information about this project:

Richard Julian
Refuge Manager
Rydell National Wildlife Refuge
Route 3, Box 105
Erskine, MN 56535
218/687-2229

John Schomaker
Project Coordinator
U.S. Fish and Wildlife Service
1 Federal Drive
Fort Snelling, MN 55111-4056
612/713-5476

I. Purpose and Need for the Proposed Action

Purpose of Action

The purpose of the proposed action is to specify a management direction for Rydell National Wildlife Refuge for the next 15 years. This management direction will be described in detail through a set of goals, objectives, and strategies in a Comprehensive Conservation Plan.

Need for Action

A long-term management direction does not currently exist for Rydell National Wildlife Refuge. Management is now guided by general policies and shorter-term plans. Also, the action is needed to address current management issues and to satisfy the legislative mandates of the National Wildlife Refuge System Improvement Act of 1997, which requires the preparation of a Comprehensive Conservation Plan for all national wildlife refuges.

Decisions that Need to be Made

The Regional Director needs to make two decisions based on this Environmental Assessment: (1) which alternative to select and (2) whether or not the selected alternative is a major Federal action significantly affecting the quality of the human environment, which would require the preparation of an environmental impact statement.

Scoping of the Issues

The Fish and Wildlife Service publicly announced it was preparing a plan for the Rydell National Wildlife Refuge in June 1996. Throughout the planning process, the Service coordinated with federal, state, and local conservation agencies, educational institutions, conservation and social action organizations, and numerous individuals who had demonstrated an interest in Refuge management activities.

Coordination also involved issuing news releases; forming a "Citizen Committee" planning team; conducting sessions with focus groups; and holding public information and input meetings.

For additional detail on these activities see Chapter 1 of the Comprehensive Conservation Plan.

Issues and Concerns

From public involvement activities, the Service learned about issues that concerned people about management of the Refuge. We organized the issues into six categories.

Water Management Many of the lakes, wetlands, and water flows in the Refuge landscape have been altered over the years for fish rearing, farming, or aesthetic purposes. Most of the alterations were completed without permits or approval from the Minnesota Department of Natural Resources. Some people strongly favor restoring the hydrologic system on the Refuge to its original character.

Removing all of the water control structures and channels on the Refuge, however, could limit some waterfowl management capabilities and hamper some fishery opportunities.

Water Quality Water quality within the Refuge, particularly in Tamarack Lake, is influenced by land management practices on lands draining into County Ditch 73. Water quality in Maple Lake, downstream of Tamarack Lake, is a major concern to local residents. Some people feel that potential projects could be identified to improve water quality and demonstrate effective water quality management practices on and off the Refuge.

Community Involvement The local community is very interested in participating in the decisions that have an impact on the future direction of the Refuge. Former landowners, volunteers, and other individuals want to contribute and be involved in Refuge management and programs. The human history of the area (settlement, reliance on the land, structures) is of special interest and should play a role in the education and interpretation programs.

Public Use Opinions vary on how to maintain the improvements made by the former owner. The improvements include trails, roads, observation structures, and buildings that provide visitor access to the Refuge. There is also concern about the level of use that would be compatible with the natural resource values of the Refuge. And, accessibility to the landscape, facilities, and programs is a major concern.

Interpretive and Educational Potential Most people support the concept of using Refuge resources and facilities to interpret the natural environment, educate about natural resources management, and demonstrate effective conservation techniques.

Habitat Restoration and Management A wide range of habitat restoration and management decisions confront Rydell National Wildlife Refuge, including: control of exotic species such as Eurasian buckthorn, spotted knapweed, reed canary grass, and leafy spurge; protection of unique natural communities such as the Sundew bog, prairie remnants, and high quality maple/basswood forests; limited habitat for forest interior species due to fragmentation of forested habitat; management and alteration of non-native plantings such as shelterbelts and conifer plantations; and distribution and quantity of grassland, forest, and wetland habitat.

Authority, Legal Compliance, and Compatibility

Authority delegated by Congress, federal regulations/guidelines, executive orders, and several management plans guide the operation and the management of the Refuge and provide the framework for the Fish and Wildlife Service's proposed action. The major laws and executive orders that apply to Rydell are listed in Appendix G of the CCP.

Background

The 2,120-acre Rydell National Wildlife Refuge is located in Grove Park and Woodside townships in Polk County, just south of U.S. Highway 2 between the communities of Mentor and Erskine, Minnesota. This area is situated in the "Prairie Pothole Region" of northwestern Minnesota between the flat Red River Valley floodplain on the west and the rolling hardwood forest and lake region on the east. In February of 1992, the land and associated facilities were sold to the Mellon Foundation, which then donated the property to the U.S. Fish & Wildlife Service to be managed as part of the National Wildlife Refuge System.

In 1991, an Environmental Assessment (EA) was completed for the establishment of the Refuge. This document addressed biological, environmental, and socioeconomic effects related to creating a National Wildlife Refuge in northwestern Minnesota. It defined the goals of the Refuge, the authorized land management practices, hunting and other public use opportunities, land acquisition, and the biological program. The impacts of three alternatives were examined and evaluated. As a result, it was determined that the establishment of the Refuge would not significantly affect the quality of the human environment within the meaning of Section 102 (2)(c) of the National Environmental Policy Act of 1969 (NEPA).

In 1996, the U.S. Fish & Wildlife Service began preparing a Comprehensive Conservation Plan for Rydell National Wildlife Refuge. The CCP is directly linked to the establishing EA but more specifically outlines the management of wildlife habitat and development of public use facilities and programs at the Refuge for the next 15 years. The plan provides a comprehensive framework for future management and identifies management strategies as well as locations and priorities for habitat and public use development. Projects are identified and described, including their purpose, the type of development or restoration, locations, and the estimated costs. In compliance with NEPA, detailed forest, wetland, grassland, cropland, fishery, water quality, community involvement, and public use management plans will be developed to provide further guidance for management activities.

It is recommended that the reader refer to the Comprehensive Conservation Plan (CCP) for Rydell National Wildlife Refuge when reviewing this Environmental Assessment. The most relevant information in the CCP is contained in Chapter 4 – Management Direction; and Chapter 5 – Plan Implementation.

We prepared this Environmental Assessment (EA) using guidelines of the National Environmental Policy Act of 1969. The Act requires us to examine the effects of proposed actions on the natural and human environment. In the following sections we describe two alternatives for future Refuge management, the environmental consequences of each alternative, and our preferred management direction. We designed the alternative as a reasonable mix of fish and wildlife habitat prescriptions and wildlife-dependent recreational opportunities, and then we selected our alternative based on its environmental consequences and its ability to achieve the Refuge's purpose.

II. Description of Alternatives

The Fish and Wildlife Service considered a range of alternatives primarily within the context of an "alternatives workshop" with the 20-member planning team. Some of these alternatives were eliminated from detailed study. The alternatives eliminated are identified below with an explanation of why they were not considered. The best ideas/alternatives that came out of the workshops were incorporated with Service concerns into the CCP, which fully describes the "preferred" or "action" alternative.

1. Alternatives Eliminated from Consideration

a) "Care-taker" Status – Refuge staff, funding, and management activities would be reduced to a level whereby the only Fish and Wildlife Service presence would be land ownership.

This alternative is not compatible with the purposes for which the Refuge was established: "for the development, advancement, management, conservation and protection of fish and wildlife resources...".

Wetland, grassland, and forest protection and restoration activities would cease. The legal responsibilities associated with ownership of the Refuge and the existing facilities, which currently includes 2,120 acres, an office, visitor center, residence, shop facility, and several other buildings, would not be met. Public recreation and interpretation programs would be curtailed on the Refuge. Protection functions, such as law enforcement, fire suppression, and cultural resources monitoring, would be limited. Commitments made to the community and support groups would be unfulfilled.

b) Manage as a Waterfowl Production Area – Refuge lands would be open to public use with limited restrictions. Hunting and trapping activities would occur over the entire Refuge. Intensive farming would continue until the area could be seeded to warm season native grasses. The buildings and other facilities would be sold and the building sites reclaimed. Wetlands would be restored as funding permitted.

This alternative is not compatible with the purpose for which the Refuge was established: "for the development, advancement, management, conservation and protection of fish and wildlife resources...". Commitments made to the community and support groups would be unfulfilled.

2. Alternatives Considered

This section describes two alternatives considered by the U.S. Fish and Wildlife Service and detailed in this Environmental Assessment:

Alternative 1 – No Action Alternative, and

Alternative 2 – Proposed Action Alternative to implement the Rydell National Wildlife Refuge Comprehensive Conservation Plan.

Alternative 1 – No Action

Present management practices continue if this Alternative is selected. The No Action alternative is a status quo alternative where current conditions and trends continue. It also serves as the baseline to compare and contrast with the other alternative.

Water Management A total of 82 wetland basins, ranging from Type I through Type VIII, are dispersed throughout the Refuge. Under this alternative, one or two wetland basins are restored each year as funding permits. Reestablishment of the natural water levels and drainage patterns on the Type IV and V brood marshes are dependent upon intermittent special funding.

Water Quality Very little time and funds are directed to off-Refuge projects that would affect the quality of water that flows into the Refuge from Ditch 73. An estimated 10 acres of the 800 acres of cropland are taken out of crop production and reestablished into native grasses each year. At this rate, the Refuge farming program continues indefinitely as a means of controlling weeds and preparing the soil for native grass seeding and continues to be a source of chemical laden water run off into Refuge wetlands and Maple Lake.

Community Involvement The current levels of coordination continue with the Minnesota Department of Natural Resources, Friends of the Rydell Refuge, University of Minnesota-Crookston, Options Resource Center for Independent Living, and several dedicated volunteers. Limited Refuge projects proposed under this alternative do not require any greater coordination.

Public Use Visitors have access to the Refuge one or two days per week as volunteers are available to staff the visitor center and for the special events that are planned and hosted by the Friends of the Rydell Refuge. Public access is limited to hiking and skiing on specific trails or short guided Refuge tours. The existing visitor facilities, such as the visitor center and Refuge office, are made accessible as funding becomes available.

Interpretive and Educational Potential The current levels of outreach, which reflect an enthusiastic staff and friends organization, continue. Refuge staff continue to assist with the interpretive and educational programs that are presently planned and hosted by the Friends of the Rydell Refuge.

Habitat Restoration and Management Ten acres of cropland are restored to native prairie grassland, 5 acres of mesic deciduous forest are reestablished, and one or two wetland basins are restored each year. The present cooperative farming program is maintained to control weeds and prepare the soil for seeding of native prairie grasses.

Management of Cultural Resources The Refuge Manager considers potential impacts of management activities on historic properties, archeological sites, traditional cultural properties, sacred sites, and human remains and cultural materials. The Refuge Manager informs the Regional Historic Preservation Officer early in the planning stage to allow qualified analysis, evaluation, consultation, and mitigation as necessary.

Archeological investigations and collecting are performed only in the public interest by qualified archeologists working under an Archaeological Resources

Protection Act permit issued by the Regional Director. Refuge personnel take steps to prevent unauthorized collecting by the public, contractors, and refuge personnel. Violations are reported to the Regional Historic Preservation Officer.

Alternative 2 – Implement the Comprehensive Conservation Plan (Preferred Alternative)

Water Management All of the drained wetland basins are restored by 2002. In addition, the natural hydrological patterns of the Refuge wetlands are reestablished, water levels in the Type IV and V marshes are lowered to maximize waterfowl brood habitat. The water level of Swan Lake is managed to provide trumpeter swan nesting habitat.

Water Quality In cooperation and partnership with the Red Lake Watershed District and the Maple Lake Improvement Association, the Refuge takes a proactive role in addressing water quality issues that originate outside of the Refuge boundary. Most of the project implementation is based on partnerships formed with landowners in the watershed, farm and conservation organizations, and with appropriate federal, state, and county agencies. Refuge staff work with private landowners, conservation organizations, and governmental agencies to bring programs into the watershed to help meet the water quality goal. Special emphasis is placed on encouraging landowners along Polk County Ditch 73 to use filter strips, grass water ways, and restore wetlands. Refuge staff restore a minimum of three wetlands and initiate at least one other conservation practice per year on private lands along Ditch 73 in connection with the Service's private lands program. The Refuge restores drained seasonal wetlands and reestablishs the natural hydrological patterns on the Refuge.

Community Involvement Refuge staff recruit a cadre of volunteers from the surrounding communities. The volunteers are trained, equipped, and enabled to become actively involved in many aspects of Refuge management. The Refuge has a self-managed volunteer program that is fully integrated into Refuge operations by the year 2012, including a paid, full-time volunteer coordinator. Community involvement in Refuge programs continues to be promoted and encouraged. The Friends of the Rydell Refuge Association assist the Refuge by seeking funding and providing assistance with the public use and educational programs. Formalized partnerships are established with conservation organizations, universities, and other local groups.

Public Use There are increased opportunities for bird watching, hunting, hiking, education, habitat restoration, and scientific study in this alternative. The emphasis in public use is increased programs and services with little new facility development. Facility changes stress accessibility. All of the existing and planned public use facilities are fully accessible for people with disabilities and meet the requirements of the American Disability Act (ADA).

Interpretive and Educational Potential Refuge staff take a lead role in providing information about wildlife, land stewardship, natural/cultural history, and educational programs. There are more outreach efforts and educational/interpretive programs. Facilities to enhance outdoor experiences throughout the Refuge include hiking/cross-country ski trails, boardwalks, observation platforms, and an auto tour route. The Refuge visitor center provides a focal point to orient and educate visitors. Special events, guided tours, educational programs, and field trips are offered to acquaint visitors with the Refuge's cultural history, natural resources, wildlife, resource issues, and management.

Habitat Restoration and Management Under this alternative, 272 acres of cropland are converted to native prairie grassland, 499 acres of mesic deciduous forest are reestablished, and all wetland basins are restored by 2002. The farming program is reduced to approximately 42 acres (see Table 1).

Management of Cultural Resources Same as alternative 1.

For a comparison of alternatives, see Table 2 on page 124.

III. Affected Environment

Historically, the area was a small forested island within the Prairie Pothole Region. A concentration of lakes to the south and west formed a "fire shadow" that supported the growth of maple-basswood and oak forest surrounded by northern tallgrass prairie. Many of the trees were cleared for farming during the homesteading era.

Today the Refuge is a mosaic of wetlands, hardwood stands, conifer plantations, grass meadows and cropland. Wetlands make up 657 acres of the Refuge; trees and shrubs about 500 acres; grassland 590 acres; and cropland constitutes 293 acres. The fragmentation of the plant communities negatively affects wildlife and ecosystem management. The area around the Refuge is dominated by agriculture with crops grown on most cleared land. In 1994 and 1995, a team of biologists from the University of Minnesota–Crookston conducted a baseline plant inventory with emphasis on native, remnant communities. The biologists concluded that "... the Refuge is in a uniquely positioned ecotonal setting on the borders of major North American biomes. Consideration should be given to looking at the entire refuge as an example of large scale ecosystem restoration with a view towards restoring a sizable unit of maple-basswood and oak forest types, particularly for forest interior species (birds and plants)." The biologists further identified Sundew Bog as the most unique remnant community on the Refuge. The biologists also recommended controlling undesirable invasive woody species such as common buckthorn and prickly ash to protect the integrity of the native communities.

The diverse Refuge habitat is currently used by diving and dabbling ducks, geese, swans, white-tailed deer, moose, ruffed grouse, cormorants, herons, rabbits, raccoon, otter, beaver, mink, muskrats, black bear, fox, coyotes, hawks, and owls. More than 195 species of birds have been observed on the Refuge. A bald eagle's nest is located approximately 1 mile south of the Refuge. And, eagles and osprey are often seen using Refuge habitat. Trumpeter swans, a state-listed threatened species, were recently reintroduced on the Refuge and now use the Refuge regularly. The Refuge is within the peripheral range of the gray wolf and unconfirmed sightings of wolves have been reported on the Refuge.

The Refuge has 24 reported cultural resources sites and 58 standing structures on Refuge land. The potential for additional cultural resources on the Refuge is mixed. Undiscovered prehistoric sites are likely, especially for the Woodland culture (500 B.C. to A.D. 1650) in this vegetative transition zone. The Cheyenne tribe is the earliest historic period tribe in the area, replaced by the Ojibwa. It is likely that all historic period sites have been located, with little potential for Indian sites and trading posts. As of September 6, 2000, Polk County contains six

Table 1: Habitat Conversion

Current Habitat Acres		Planned Habitat Acres							
		Lakes	Wetlands and Wet Meadows	Grassland/ Wetland Complex	Grass/Shrub Complex	Maple, Basswood and Oak Forest	Agricultural Fields	Conifer Demonstration	Facilities Development
Lakes	232	232							
Wetlands	338		188	39	28	88			
Hardwood	419		9	15	26	365			
Conifer Plantations	135		3	25	16	86		5	
Grass Meadows	489		12	220	88	163		4	
Cropland	272			115		116	42		
Facilities/ Development	26								26
Grassland/ Wetland Complex	85		24	11	33	17			
Grass/Shrub Complex	11		2	3		6			
Total Acres	**2,007***	**232**	**238**	**428**	**191**	**841**	**42**	**9**	**26**

* Total acres do not equate total legal acreage (2,120) due to lack of precision of GIS at the scale digitized.

Table 2 – Comparison of Alternatives (By Year 2012)

Issues and Concerns	Alternative 1 No Action	Alternative 2 Implement CCP
1. Water Management	Restore 1 or 2 wetlands per year as funding permits.	Restore all drained wetlands by 2002; reestablish the natural hydrological patterns of Refuge Wetlands.
2. Water Quality	Restore 1 or 2 wetlands per year as funding permits.	Restore 5 undrained wetlands per year; reestablish the natural hydrological patterns of Refuge wetlands; work with Watershed District, Ditch 73 authority, and landowners to reduce phosphorous and nitrate loads entering the Refuge and Maple Lake.
3. Community Involvement	Maintain coordination; maintain current partners.	Establish self-managed and funded volunteer program; formalize educational, accessibility, and research partnerships.
4. Public Use	Maintain 2,500 visits per year; maintain existing public use facilities.	Meet the needs of 5,000 to 7,000 visitors per year; make existing and new facilities fully accessible.
5. Interpretive and Educational Potential	Maintain existing interpretive and educational programs.	Formalize educational partnerships with surrounding schools and universities; develop fully accessible interpretive displays, trails, and overlooks; provide environmental education programs; promote "Watchable Wildlife" program.
6. Habitat Restoration and Management	Restore 5 acres of mesic and decidous forest, 10 acres of native prairie grassland, and 1 or 2 wetlands per year. Maintain farming program to control weeds.	Restore 499 acres of mesic and decidous forest, 20 acres of native prairie grassland and all wetlands. All wetlands restored by 2002. Farming program of 42 acres for wildlife viewing.

properties on the National Register of Historic Places. All these properties are historic period structures located in cities. To date, two cultural resources investigations have produced artifacts from Refuge lands; these collections are stored at the Minnesota Historical Society under a cooperative agreement.

IV. Environmental Consequences

Effects Common to Both Alternatives

Under both alternatives, the Service obligations for Cultural Resources Management, Threatened and Endangered Species, and other legal mandates will be met.

Because of the location and type of activities proposed for the comprehensive conservation plan, there will be "no affect" on the bald eagle, gray wolf or any other federally listed threatened or endangered species or their critical habitat.

The following section evaluates the impacts that the two alternatives would have on the six issues/concerns that were identified in the CCP.

Alternative 1 – No Action

Water Management It could take up to 25 years for the Refuge to reach its full waterfowl production capability. Invertebrate populations in Clifford Lake may be decreased and waterfowl productivity may be less than full potential. We would not know the effect of rearing walleye without an evaluation study.

Water Quality The Refuge farming program would continue indefinitely. The farming program and farming upstream would continue to be a source of chemical laden water run off into Refuge wetlands and Maple Lake. Algae growth would continue and, as a result, the supply of oxygen necessary to fish would continue to be depleted, and the aquatic food chain would continue to be disrupted.

Community Involvement The Refuge presence in the local communities would be maintained but not expanded.

Public Use The estimated visitation in 15 years would be around 5,000 visitors per year. The wildlife and other Refuge natural resources may benefit from limited public use. Disturbance to wildlife would be minimal and habitat would not be displaced for access, education, and other facilities. Much of the Refuge would continue to be inaccessible to the disabled public. The Refuge would not be able to provide sufficient public access to its lands to generate long-term public support. Local communities and tourism groups would not actively promote and identify their relationship with the Refuge. Over the long-term, this would translate into inadequate funding and reduced partnerships because of reduced public support.

Interpretive and Educational Potential Current local support and understanding would continue with moderate increases over time. Negative impacts on wildlife and habitat would be minimal.

Habitat Restoration and Management It would take up to 25 years to restore all of the wetland basins, plant 400 acres of forest, and establish 300 acres of native prairie grassland on the Refuge. The full wildlife production and maintenance potential of the Refuge would not be realized until all the restoration projects were completed. There would be very little change to waterfowl production, neotropical migratory bird use, and resident wildlife populations in the short-term. The status of any threatened or endangered species would remain unchanged.

Alternative 2 – Implement the Comprehensive Conservation Plan (Preferred Alternative)

Water Management The waterfowl production potential of the Refuge would be increased considerably. Restoring the natural hydrological patterns and levels for most of the Type IV and V wetlands would rectify the illegal alterations that were completed prior to the area becoming a national wildlife refuge. The effect of rearing walleye fry in Clifford Lake would be studied.

Water Quality Water quality of wetland habitat on the Refuge and especially Maple Lake would improve. Algae growth in the lakes would decrease, the supply of oxygen for fish would increase, and the aquatic food chain would be more intact in the lakes. Landowners within the Red Lake Watershed District would likely be more knowledgeable and active in protecting the water quality of the area.

Community Involvement The Refuge would experience an ever increasing base of support. The Friends of the Rydell Refuge Association would assist the Refuge by seeking funding and providing assistance with the public use and educational programs. People in the surrounding communities would help promote a sense of ownership. The Refuge would receive recognition and support for funding during the next 15 years.

Public Use The Refuge would attract additional visitors who are interested in bird watching, hunting, hiking, education, habitat restoration, and scientific study. Public use visits to the Refuge would increase, and visitors would have a higher quality experience. The Refuge visitors' awareness of the natural world would increase and this would translate into increased public support for the Refuge. Increased visitation would lead to increased spending in the local economy. The negative impacts of increased public use on the Refuge would include a greater potential for wildlife disturbance by the public, increased maintenance and operating costs to build and maintain public use facilities, and wildlife habitat displacement by access and recreational facilities. Negative impacts from public use would be alleviated through stipulations made in compatibility determinations for each use.

Interpretive and Educational Potential Visitors would develop a better understanding of their dependence on the natural environment and the management techniques employed to protect and restore natural systems. Increased visitor contacts would increase public support for the Refuge and increase long-term spending in the local economy. The negative impacts of increased programs for the public would include a greater potential for wildlife disturbance by the public, increased maintenance and operating costs to build and maintain educational and interpretation facilities, and wildlife habitat displacement by access and education facilities.

Habitat Restoration and Management The conversion of crop land and conifer plantations to reconstructed native habitats would have a net positive effect on the physical and biological resources. Conversion of cropland would reduce soil erosion, reduce the use of chemicals, and increase biodiversity. The restored native plant communities would afford greater protection and enhancement for the animal populations that utilize those habitats. Increased grassland acres would provide additional cover for geese and nesting habitat for mallards. The increased grassland acres would also benefit the following birds with special regional status: American black duck; blue-winged teal; northern pintail; bald eagle; northern harrier; northern goshawk; peregrine falcon; field sparrow; grasshopper sparrow; bobolink; and eastern meadowlark. (See Appendix F for a more complete listing of wildlife species and their habitats.) More acres and larger blocks of deciduous forest would benefit the following birds with special regional status: wood ducks; northern goshawk; peregrine falcon; American woodcock; yellow-billed cuckoo; northern flicker; Acadian flycatcher; veery;

chesnut-sided warbler; field sparrow; and grasshopper sparrow. The loss of even-aged conifer plantations would have a small effect on a few species of songbirds that may use the trees for cover, but none of these birds are solely dependent upon the conifers. The status of any threatened or endangered species would not be negatively affected, and it may be enhanced through more natural habitat. Cultural resources would be afforded more protection, because the soil would be disturbed less.

Table 3: Summary of Consequences Under Alternatives

Issues and Opportunities	Alternative 1 No Action	Alternative2 Implement the CCP (Preferred Alternative)
Water Management	May take 25 years to reach full waterfowl production potential. Invertebrate and waterfowl productivity may be suppressed in Clifford Lake.	Waterfowl production potential increased considerably within 3 years. Effect of rearing walleye in Clifford Lake would be better understood.
Water Quality	Algae growth in lakes with fewer fish and disruption in aquatic food chain.	Decreased algae growth in lakes, healthy fish populations, and healthy aquatic food chain.
Community Involvement	Current base of support for the Refuge would be maintained.	Increased base of support for the Refuge.
Public Use	Visitation would increase moderately. Disturbance to wildlife would be minimal. Low community identity with the Refuge.	Increased visitation with higher quality visitor experiences. Greater potential for wildlife disturbance. Increased spending in the local economy. Increased support for the Refuge.
Interpretive and Educational Potential	Current local support would continue. Negative impacts on wildlife and habitat would be minimal.	Increased understanding of environment. Increased public support. Greater potential for wildlife disturbance.
Habitat Restoration and Management	Little change in waterfowl production, neotropical migratory bird use, and resident wildlife populations.	Reduced soil erosion. Increased biodiversity. Enhanced wildlife populations.
Management of Cultural Resources	Cultural resources protected.	Cultural resources protected.
Threatened and Endangered Species	No increase in threats.	No increase in threats; more natural habitat would enhance habitat for greater diversity of species.

V. List of Preparers

Rick Julian
Refuge Manager, Rydell National Wildlife Refuge

B.S. in Fish and Wildlife Management, University of Minnesota, St. Paul, 3 years as Wildlife Technician Minnesota Section of Game, conducting grouse research on the Red Lake Wildlife Management Area, Warroad, Minnesota. Three years as Fishery Biologist on Great Lakes Research Vessel Cisco with Great Lakes Fishery Laboratory, Ann Arbor, Michigan. Eight years as Fish and Wildlife Biologist at the East Lansing Ecological Field Office, Michigan, 11 years with Division of Federal as Regional 3 Hunter Education Specialist and Wildlife Section Supervisor, Fort Snelling, Minnesota. Five years as Manager of the Detroit Lakes Wetland Management District and Rydell Refuge, Detroit Lakes, Minnesota, and one year as project manager Glacial Ridge project and Refuge Manager for Rydell National Wildlife Refuge, Erskine, Minnesota.

Les Peterson
Wildlife Biologist, Detroit Lakes Wetland Management District

B.S. in wildlife science, Utah State University, Logan, Utah. Biological Technician at San Bernard National Wildlife Refuge in 1978; between 1978 and 1986, served as Assistant Manager at Brazoria National Wildlife Refuge, Aransas National Wildlife Refuge in charge of Matagorda Island, Havasu National Wildlife Refuge in charge of the Bill Williams Unit, and the Lacrosse District of the Upper Mississippi River National Wildlife & Fish Refuge; in 1986 transferred to the Detroit Lakes Wetland Management District as Assistant Wetland Manager; Wildlife Biologist at the Wetland Management District since 1990.

John Schomaker
Project Coordinator, U.S. Fish and Wildlife Service Great Lakes-Big Rivers Regional Office

B.A. in chemistry, Carleton College, Northfield, Minnesota; M.S. in Outdoor Recreation, Utah State University, Logan, Utah; Ph.D. in Recreation Management, Colorado State University, Fort Collins, Colorado. Three years teaching and conducting research in wildland recreation and wilderness management, University of Idaho, Moscow, Idaho; 8 years in river recreation research for North Central Forest Experiment Station, U.S. Forest Service, St. Paul, Minnesota; 10 years as recreation planner at Minnesota Valley NWR, Bloomington, Minnestoa; 4 years as refuge planner for Region 3, U.S. Fish and Wildlife Service, Fort Snelling, Minnesota.

Appendix J: Mailing List

Appendix J: Mailing List

Federal Officials

U.S. Senator Mark Dayton
U.S. Senator Paul Wellstone
U.S. Representative Collin Peterson

Federal Agencies

USDA/ Natural Resource Conservation Service
USDI/ Fish & Wildlife Service, Albuquerque, New Mexico; Anchorage, Alaska; Atlanta, Georgia; Denver, Colorado; Fort Snelling, Minnesota; Hadley, Massachusetts; Portland, Oregon; Washington, D.C.

State Officials

Governor Jesse Ventura
Senator Roger Moe
Representative Bernie Lieder

State Agencies

Commissioner Allen Garber, Minnesota Department of Natural Resources
Terry Wolfe, District Manager, Minnesota Department of Natural Resources
State Historic Preservation Officer, St. Paul, Minnesota
Minnesota Environmental Quality Board
Dan Svedarsky, Fish and Wildlife Department, University of Minnesota–Crookston

City/County/Township Governments

Mayor, City of Erskine
Mayor, City of Mentor
City Administrator, City of Crookston
Polk County Board of Commissioners
Woodside Township Board of Supervisors
Grove Park Township Board of Supervisors

Tribes

Red Lake Band of Chippewa

Organizations

Friends of Rydell National Wildlife Refuge Association
The Nature Conservancy
Richard King Mellon Foundation
Minnesota Deer Hunters Association
Minnesota Waterfowl Association
Pheasants Forever
Ruffed Grouse Society
National Audubon Society
Ducks Unlimited
Wildlife Management Institute
PEER Refuge Keeper
The Wilderness Society, Washington, D.C.
National Wildlife Federation
Sierra Club, Midwest Office, Madison, Wisconsin
The National Wildlife Refuge Association, Washington, D.C.
The Conservation Fund, Arlington, Virginia
Polk County Historical Society
Wildlife Society, Minnesota Chapter

Media

Erskine Echo
Crookston Daily News
Outdoor News
KQHt FM 96.1, Grand Forks, North Dakota
KROX AM 1260, Crookston, Minnesota
Twin Valley Times
Norman County Index
Thirteen Towns
Fargo Forum
Minneapolis/St. Paul StarTribune
St. Paul Pioneer Press
Grand Forks Herald
Northern Watch
KKAQ, Foston, Minnesota
KKCQ, Foston, Minnesota
KXJO, Fargo/Grand Forks
KVLY, Fargo/Grand Forks
KFGO, Fargo
WDAY/WDAZ, Fargo/Grand Forks
KCNN AM 590, Grand Forks

Individuals

Individuals who participated in open houses or who have requested to be on the mailing list for the Rydell National Wildlife Refuge CCP.

Appendix K: List of Preparers

Appendix K: List of Preparers

Rick Julian
Refuge Manager
Rydell NWR, Erskine, Minn.

Mr. Julian provided overall direction, supervision and coordination with agencies and the public. He contributed to writing and editing the CCP.

John Schomaker
Refuge Planning Specialist
Regional Office, Fort Snelling, Minn.

Mr. Schomaker provided coordination and served as co-author of the CCP.

John Dobrovolny
Regional Historian
Regional Office, Fort Snelling, Minn.

Mr. Dobrovolny is the primary author of cultural resource sections.

Sean Killen
Cartographer
Regional Office, Fort Snelling, Minn.

Mr. Killen assisted with the preparation of maps.

Jane Hodgins
Technical Writer/Editor
Regional Office, Fort Snelling, Minn.

Ms. Hodgins served as primary editor of the CCP.

Appendix K: Summary and Disposition of Public Comments on the Draft CCP

Appendix L: Summary and Disposition of Public Comments on Draft Comprehensive Conservation Plan

One government agency and three individuals – one person via email and two persons orally at an open house – commented on the Draft Comprehensive Conservation Plan.

We considered the comments as we prepared the final Comprehensive Conservation Plan. The following paragraphs describe the comments and our response.

A comment from Region 5 of the Environmental Protection Agency encouraged us to consider expanding the range of alternatives in the Environmental Assessment. The suggestion was to include one alternative that focuses on serving recreation use needs in the national wildlife refuge versus a focus on restoration of historic ecosystem types and another alternative that might balance recreation and restoration through adaptive management.

In the Environmental Assessment we describe two other alternatives that we considered but did not develop further and the reasons why we did not pursue them. In our view, Alternative 2 (Preferred Alternative) represents the alternative suggested as a balance of recreation and restoration. The suggestion to consider an alternative that focuses on serving recreation needs in the Refuge runs counter to the "wildlife first" direction within the National Wildlife Refuge System Improvement Act of 1997. In general, the system at Rydell National Wildlife Refuge is simple and the issues and needs are not complex. For all of these reasons, we feel that the two alternatives that we developed and compared are adequate.

Individuals wanted the plan to clarify use regulations related to snowmobiling, canoeing, and rollerblading. These uses are prohibited and we have made this explicit in the final plan.

An individual questioned the need for the proposed auto tour route given the amount of paved trails and the availability of golf carts that provide access to persons with mobility needs. The individual suggested that an alternative would be to route a one-way auto tour from east to west through the Refuge past the demonstration area and out the west side of the Refuge. This route would eliminate the northern loop proposed in the plan. We think the alternative route merits consideration. We will consider and evaluate this alternative route when a detailed public use plan is drafted and the engineering, construction, and public use aspects are developed more fully.

Individuals also commented on the need for a date change for the beginning of the fishery study, tree removal at the entrance road, and the need to reduce the number of deer on the Refuge and the possibility of a bounty. The date for the fishery study has been changed in the final plan. The comment on tree removal was based on a misunderstanding of the plan and did not necessitate a change in the plan. Deer management on the Refuge is coordinated with the State of Minnesota and conducted under their regulations. We think the possibility of using a bounty as an incentive for deer removal is very low. In the context of adaptive management, we will monitor the effects of the CCP's objective 1.9 that sets the level of the Refuge's deer population.